Multicast Sockets

Practical Guide for Programmers

David Makofske

Akamai Technologies

Kevin Almeroth

University of California, Santa Barbara

MORGAN KAUFMANN PUBLISHERS

AN IMPRINT OF ELSEVIER SCIENCE

AMSTERDAM   BOSTON   LONDON   NEW YORK
OXFORD   PARIS   SAN DIEGO   SAN FRANCISCO
SINGAPORE   SYDNEY   TOKYO

Senior Editor   Rick Adams
Publishing Services Manager   Edward Wade
Senior Production Editor   Cheri Palmer
Developmental Editor   Karyn Johnson
Cover Design   Yvo Riezebos
Cover Image   © PhotoDisc/GettyImages
Text Design   Side by Side Studios/Mark Ong
Composition and Illustration   Windfall Software, using ZzTeX
Copyeditor   Robert Fiske
Proofreader   Mary Roybal
Indexer   Bill Meyer
Printer   The Maple-Vail Book Manufacturing Group

Designations used by companies to distinguish their products are often claimed as trademarks or registered trademarks. In all instances in which Morgan Kaufmann Publishers is aware of a claim, the product names appear in initial capital or all capital letters. Readers, however, should contact the appropriate companies for more complete information regarding trademarks and registration.

Morgan Kaufmann Publishers
An imprint of Elsevier Science
340 Pine Street, Sixth Floor
San Francisco, CA 94104-3205
www.mkp.com

07   06   05   04   03   5   4   3   2   1

Library of Congress Control Number: 2002108513
ISBN: 1-55860-846-X

This book is printed on acid-free paper.

This book is dedicated to our wives,
without whose love and support this project
would probably never have been finished.

Contents

Preface   ix

1   Introduction   1
1.1   Multicast Defined   2
1.2   Unicast vs. Multicast vs. Broadcast   2
1.3   The Multicast Trade-off: Power/Flexibility vs. Complexity   3
1.4   An Overview of Multicast Protocols   5
1.5   Organization of This Book   7
1.6   Exercises   7

2   Multicasting with C Sockets   9
2.1   UDP Sockets   9
2.2   Sending Multicast Packets in C   10
2.3   Receiving Multicast Packets in C   22
2.4   A Sample Run of Sender and Receiver(s)   30
2.5   C and Source Specific Multicast   31
2.6   Winsock Modifications   31
2.7   Exercises   32

3   Multicasting with Java   33
3.1   The Java MulticastSocket API   33
3.2   A Java Multicast Sender   34
3.3   Receiving Multicast Packets in Java   42
3.4   A Sample Run   49
3.5   Exercises   49

4   Multicasting with .NET   51
4.1   The .NET Sockets Class   51
4.2   Sending Multicast Packets in C#   52

4.3   Receiving Multicast Packets in C#   61
4.4   A Sample Run: C# Multicast Sender and Receiver   70
4.5   C# and Source Specific Multicast   70
4.6   The C# UdpClient Class   71
4.7   Exercises   76

5   **Source Specific Multicast   77**
5.1   Source Specific Multicast Defined   77
5.2   Advantages of SSM   78
5.3   Host Support for SSM   80
5.4   SSM Additions to the APIs   80
5.5   Exercises   85

6   **Multicast Addressing and Scoping   87**
6.1   Scoping   87
6.2   Multicast Address Space   90
6.3   Selecting a Multicast Address   92
6.4   Java Multicast Address Scope Methods   93
6.5   Exercises   94

7   **Multicast Reachability and Scalability   95**
7.1   Multicast Reachability   95
7.2   Multicast Ping   97
7.3   Multicast Scalability   113
7.4   MPing with Receiver-Based Congestion Control   116
7.5   Exercises   126

8   **Application-Layer Multicast and Reflectors   127**
8.1   Introduction   127
8.2   A Multicast Reflector in Java   128
8.3   Exercises   149

9   **Summarizing Lessons Learned   151**

Appendix A   **Multicast History and Protocols   155**
A.1   Multicast Service Models   155
A.2   The Evolution of Multicast   157

Appendix B   **Summary of Multicast API by Language   169**

References   173

Index   176

Preface

As new technologies are incorporated into the Internet infrastructure, the once impossible will become possible. As an example, the World Wide Web (WWW) was once "just" used to locate and retrieve documents. Now it is a media-rich environment for interacting in a global online community. To support the as-yet unimagined applications of tomorrow, better, more sophisticated technology is needed today.

One-to-many communication, called multicast, is one of the first services to improve on the nearly ageless—in Internet years at least—Internet Protocol (IP). Instead of just best-effort delivery of packets, multicast provides the ability to send one packet and have it reach potentially millions of users. Multicast stands poised to revolutionize the kinds of applications offered on the Internet. Without multicast, one-to-many applications like streaming Internet radio, Video-on-Demand (VoD), Internet-based video jukeboxes, and videoconferencing are almost impossible to provide.

In order for Internet users to have the opportunity to experience these new applications, multicast needs to be incorporated into the infrastructure and into applications. Programmers must know how to create sockets capable of delivering a single transmitted packet to potentially millions of group members. Fortunately, multicast was designed in such a way that the Application Programming Interface (API) is not significantly different from the unicast API. Details of the actual mechanisms to accomplish one-to-many delivery are hidden in the network. And because several books already focus on the intricacies of deploying multicast in a network, this book focuses on approaching multicast from an application programmer's point of view.

Luckily, because of the power of network abstraction, an application programmer need not know much about what happens in the network (though, what basic knowledge is useful is covered in this book). Instead, the real challenge for an application programmer is to get beyond the basics of multicast socket syntax and to understand the problems and solutions of using multicast in applications. The differences between using unicast and using multicast are as significant as the differences between talking in a one-on-one meeting and effectively lecturing to a room full of people. This book's goal is to create the multicast equivalent of outstanding public speakers.

Intended Audience

Because multicast is a relatively new technology, this book is intended for anyone who is interested in experimenting with multicast sockets and applications. As just mentioned, while there are other books that focus on the network administration side of multicast, this book is tailored toward the needs of application programmers.

In order to effectively use this book, you need to have sound programming skills, including some basic knowledge of sockets. Most any language will do. In fact, this book presents basic examples in three core languages: C, Java, and C#. Additional, extended examples are presented in one of these three languages. As the book's Web site evolves, we expect not only to include new examples, but to offer them in all three languages.

Approach

This book attempts to balance a basic description of multicast and how it works with coding examples that teach programmers how to write multicast sockets. As such, there is something of an ideological conflict: present all the background material and then give code examples versus using the code examples to drive the explanation. We have settled on the latter.

Although Chapter 1 contains enough information to get started in writing multicast sockets, it has barely an overview of the basics of multicast. Much of what a programmer needs to know is therefore contained in Appendix A. Anyone interested in a better understanding of how multicast works should read Appendix A before advancing too far into the book.

With Chapters 2 through 4, we jump directly into the code. All three chapters offer the same basic multicast sender and receiver example but in three different languages. Again, the choice we had to make was whether to present some key background concepts on multicast or whether to jump right into the code. Again, full steam ahead on the coding examples! A discussion on socket-related details with particular importance to multicast like the Time-To-Live (TTL) field, group addressing, and multicast service models are left for later chapters.

Chapters 5 and 6 go back and give a more in-depth treatment of the role of TTL and addressing in multicast. Also, Chapter 6 deals with variations on the basic multicast service model. With the basic syntactical knowledge learned in Chapters 2 through 4, these concepts make much better sense.

Chapters 7 and 8 introduce more advanced concepts in multicast—topics that are created only when one-to-many communication is used. Here, we adopt the strategy of giving background on these topics (scalability, reachability, and reflectors) while offering code that implements basic solutions to these problems.

chapter **1**

Introduction

From the birth of the Internet, the network has had significant advances in technology, rich new applications, and the evolution of networking protocols. From a network of just a few nodes, the Internet has evolved into an infrastructure critical to the world economy.

Even though there has been tremendous change, very little of it has been exposed to the application programmer. In a sense, this is a good thing. No matter how the network changes, delivery of packets is still accomplished. This is due in part to the power of network sockets. This abstract interface between application programmers and the network has been successful in protecting programmers from the details and underlying complexities of the network. Through layering and abstraction, application programmers have been able to send data across the network without worrying about the details of actual delivery of data across the various network hops. It is only through different *types* of sockets that different services are made available to a programmer.

Through transport layer protocols like the Transmission Control Protocol (TCP) and the User Datagram Protocol (UDP), different delivery services are available. UDP is very simple and only provides a programmer with port numbers. Port numbers provide multiplexing and demultiplexing; that is, ports allow different applications to keep their packets separate even though they use the same underlying delivery infrastructure. TCP is a more feature-rich protocol than UDP. TCP not only provides multiplexing and demultiplexing but also provides connection management, in-order delivery of packets, reliability, and congestion control. TCP is useful for applications like the Web and email, which fundamentally work by reliably delivering objects or files. UDP is more often used for more delay-sensitive but often more loss-tolerant applications (e.g., streaming audio and video).

And yet, even with TCP and UDP, there is still a need for more advanced functionality *inside* the network. Without advances at the network layer, neither TCP nor UDP can provide efficient, highly scalable packet delivery to a large group of users. What is needed is the ability for an application to deliver one copy of a packet to a socket, and then have the host and the network efficiently deliver that packet to all interested receivers. What is needed is multicast.

1.1 Multicast Defined

Multicast communication gives the application programmer the ability to open a UDP socket and send a packetized chunk of data once. And yet the packet is delivered to potentially many receivers. Instead of sending N separate but identical packets to each of N receivers, one multicast packet can be sent that will reach all N receivers, even if N is large.

A special range of IP addresses is used to create a logical group of receivers. Using this address, the application programmer has the ability to send one or a stream of packets to this destination address and expect the network to attempt to deliver a copy of the packet to each receiver in the multicast group.

Multicast communication relies on additional functionality in the network to build a "multicast forwarding tree" between the sending application and the group of receivers. The concept of a tree is an accurate one. The source is located at the "root" of the tree. From the root, a packet stream flows up the trunk to "branches." At each branch in the tree, the network receives an incoming packet and copies it to each of the outgoing branches. For an example of a multicast tree, see Figure 1.1.

The functionality necessary to build and maintain multicast trees for a group of receivers is slowly being deployed throughout the Internet. Deployment means that additional functionality, using additional software and/or hardware, is being deployed in Internet switches and routers as well as in host operating systems and applications. Deployment also means that there are programmers who are using multicast as an effective technique in building large-scale distributed applications. For an application programmer, using multicast means understanding the syntactic changes to the socket Application Programming Interface (API) as well as understanding the implications of using such a powerful communication mechanism.

1.2 Unicast vs. Multicast vs. Broadcast

As a former colleague once stated, "terminology is 85% of the game." This is especially true when learning a new technology. Even though multicast has been around for a number of years, many people are unfamiliar with what it is. Therefore, it is important to define what multicast is.

The terms *unicast* and *multicast* make the most sense when also considering the more common term *broadcast*. Where broadcast means to send to everyone, for example, radio, television, satellite, and so on, the other two terms cover a more restrained set of receivers. Unicast is the opposite of broadcast and means that a transmission is sent to only one user, hence "uni-" (one) combined with "-cast" (to send). Multicast is therefore the transmission to "multi-", that is, more than one but not everyone.

In the radio or television world, a broadcast does not truly go to everyone. In most broadcasts, each station has a "footprint" in which its signal can be received. This footprint is considered the entire network, and so every user has the potential to receive this signal. Television uses a combination of satellites, relays, cable plants, and so on to create a broadcast network. Traditional broadcast networks are designed to efficiently deliver a signal to everyone. While they can also technically deliver a unicast transmission—by sending a broadcast signal but expecting only one user to receive and process the data—the signal itself is not truly unicast. Multicast in these networks is accomplished the same way: a broadcast signal is sent to everyone, but only a subset of receivers is expected to receive and process the signal.

The Internet was initially designed to have unicast capability Internet-wide and a broadcast facility locally. Broadcast is frequently used in Local Area Networks (LANs). For example, *Shared Ethernet* is a broadcast protocol. Every frame sent on an Ethernet segment is broadcast across the entire medium. Each receiver uses its Medium Access Control (MAC) address to determine whether the frame is for it or not. If not, the frame is discarded. For those who are truly detail oriented, there are two types of Ethernet. Shared Ethernet is truly broadcast oriented. It is rapidly being replaced with *Switched Ethernet*. In Switched Ethernet, collisions are avoided by using a star topology in combination with buffering. Also, switches snoop on MAC addresses and avoid broadcasting by sending frames on the precise outgoing switch port. Even in the switched environment, there is often a need to send frames to all LAN hosts.

To go further into this topic would require us to explain how multicast trees are created and maintained, and how the protocols work. Though an understanding of these functions is important and is something we discuss further in Section 1.4 and Appendix A, the immediate goal is to understand what multicast is and what its benefits are.

1.3   The Multicast Trade-off: Power/Flexibility vs. Complexity

Multicast offers a great deal of power. The ability for a host to send one packet and have it potentially received by any number of receiving hosts is very powerful. More specifically, the power in multicast is its scalability. For applications that must deliver data to a large number of receivers, unicast fails quickly. Whether it is stock quotes to millions or MPEG-2 streams to a few, the bandwidth consumed in replicating a packet will almost always cause congestion. Unicast replication and a multicast tree are shown in Figure 1.1.

Multicast scalability is a great feature, but the benefits are not without a cost. The trade-off is complexity. It comes at a price for both those who must deploy multicast in the network

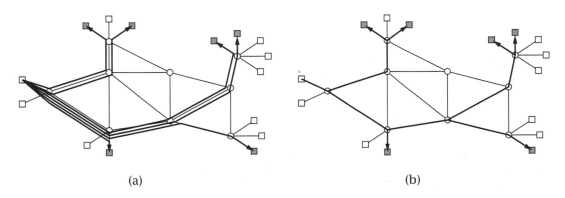

(a)   (b)

Figure 1.1 The scalability of multicast (b) over unicast (a).

and application writers. The complexities of deployment and network management are left to those who have to administer the network and so are beyond the scope of this book. Instead, we focus on what application programmers must deal with.

The complexity with multicast comes from the fact that it is essentially only a delivery mechanism. At the transport layer, multicast works only with UDP. It does not work with TCP. And as it stands, UDP generally has a poor reputation in the Internet community. It does not have congestion control, does not have a reliable delivery mechanism, and is often used to stream high-bandwidth data like audio and video. And worst of all, UDP is often used to exploit numerous security holes and perpetuate denial-of-service attacks. As a result, some security-conscious enterprises use firewalls to block all UDP traffic or allow traffic over only a small subset of ports, for example, port 53 for the Domain Name System (DNS). The consequence is that UDP traffic is sometimes blocked at firewalls.

Application programmers who would rather avoid the overhead of TCP are still sometimes forced to use fall-back strategies like using TCP or, even worse, tunneling traffic in the HyperText Transfer Protocol (HTTP). Furthermore, because unchecked congestion can cause harm not only to the Internet but also to the offending application, programmers are typically forced to implement at least some basic form of congestion control. This also implies building a back channel for collecting feedback and implementing a relatively sophisticated bandwidth adjustment mechanism (something we talk about in Chapter 7). While the academic literature is full of research proposing various techniques to do this, very few real-world UDP applications implement such sophisticated and complex algorithms.

In addition to congestion control, some applications need reliability, too. Why not use TCP then if an application writer needs a transport layer protocol that implements congestion control and reliability? Because many of the applications that run on top of UDP need reliability but not the kind of reliability offered by TCP. The way that TCP repairs lost packets is to stop transmitting new packets (within a certain window) and retransmit the lost packet(s). Once lost packets are retransmitted, received, and acknowledged, TCP is allowed to continue with the transmission of new data. For some applications (e.g., delay sensitive but not loss sensitive), this is not always desirable. For multicast-based applications, the problems are even worse. Because a source is trying to provide a single stream for group members, it becomes almost impossible to adjust to individual group member delay, loss, and jitter characteristics, especially when these can vary widely.

Consider the complexity of adding congestion control and reliability into UDP. Creating and managing all the state variables and timers quickly becomes a significant burden. Now consider what would happen if instead of one receiver there were hundreds, or thousands, or even millions. Would the application have a different sending rate for each receiver? Obviously not, since then it is not using multicast anymore. So how does a multicast sender establish a single rate that satisfies receivers connected by 56 kbps modems, cable modems, or Ethernet? How should the application handle reliability? Not only does feedback collection require significant effort (collecting an acknowledgment for every packet sent to every receiver), but how should the sending host deal with retransmissions? Should the sender resend to every receiver or just to those who lost the particular packet? The complexity of multicast-based applications comes not in sending the data, but in managing the communication.

But we have digressed into describing the really hard problems. Luckily, as a place to start, opening a multicast socket and sending datagrams is almost identical to opening a unicast UDP socket. The additional complexity comes in making sure communication can take place according to the needs of the application. This boils down to two tasks. The first has to do with ensuring that there is multicast connectivity between the sender and all the receivers and dealing with the situation when there is not always multicast connectivity but communication is still needed. The second is providing transport functionality such as reliability, congestion control, and scalable feedback. These topics are the focus of the second half of this book. The first half deals with the creation of multicast sockets in a variety of programming languages.

1.4   An Overview of Multicast Protocols

The history of multicast has been an evolution consisting of many changes. Though it is beyond the scope of this book to go into much detail, we will discuss briefly how multicast operates. For a slightly more detailed and technical description, see Appendix A.

The first deployment of multicast occurred in 1992. The motivation was to transmit audio and video from the March Internet Engineering Task Force (IETF) meeting where the development of multicast was being standardized. To prototype and deploy multicast was an excellent proof-of-concept test. Most significant about this first deployment is that there was no support in the network; it was all done at the application layer by end hosts acting as multicast routers. The idea was that multicast packets would be tunneled through the Internet by encapsulating them inside another IP packet, only this time with a unicast destination. Multicast routing software, called *mrouted* (pronounced "m-route-d"), running at the destination would strip off the encapsulation and then look at the group address. Mrouted's algorithm would identify the set of outgoing tunnels, and the packet would be replicated for each tunnel, again being encapsulated with the destination as the other end of the tunnel. Essentially, the Multicast Backbone, or MBone, was the first overlay network in the Internet. As time went on, multicast routing support was included in more and more Internet switches and routers.

For an application writer and someone dealing with sockets, an understanding of multicast routing protocols is not absolutely required. As an analogy, someone writing an application using TCP sockets does not have to know about or worry about the operation of the Border Gateway Protocol (BGP) or the Open Shortest Path First (OSPF) protocol. However, an understanding of these protocols, especially in the case of multicast, is important for understanding how to write robust applications. Instead of spending the next several chapters explaining the operation of multicast-related protocols, we provide a relatively detailed description in Appendix A. At this point, though, we provide a very brief description of what happens once a multicast socket is opened.

The first step in creating an efficient one-to-many distribution tree for a multicast group is to get information about the existence of group members to routers. The router closest to a receiver is called a leaf router. A host communicates the fact that it has joined a group and

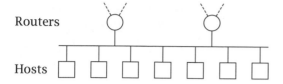

Figure 1.2 Communicating over a LAN using broadcast/multicast.

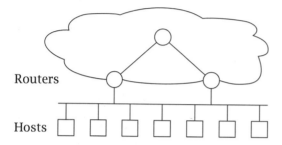

Figure 1.3 The need for a multicast routing protocol.

is expecting to receive group traffic using the Internet Group Management Protocol [11, 20, 8]. In fact, all hosts on a LAN segment use IGMP to communicate when they join or leave a group. Figure 1.2 shows a representation of a LAN segment.

As you will see, doing multicast across a LAN is very simple. This is because link-layer broadcast is already a commonly used service and no additional multicast protocols are needed. For example, the Address Resolution Protocol (ARP) broadcasts a message asking for the Medium Access Control (MAC) address for a host with a particular IP address. Multicast simply uses a group address as the destination address, and so a host joining a group will simply start listening for packets with that address.

Once a router is aware that there are hosts connected to it that want to receive particular multicast groups, it needs to graft itself into the multicast tree. The router accomplishes this function by sending join messages to adjacent routers. Figure 1.3 shows a representation of the network behind the LAN and the fact that there are multiple routers. Using this figure along with Figure 1.1, you can get a sense of the process of grafting new links when new hosts join a group and pruning useless links when hosts leave a group.

Whole additional levels of complexity are added when consideration is given for exactly how the tree should be formed and how trees are built across inter-domain boundaries. This kind of detail, including the specific protocols and their features, is relegated to Appendix A. Suffice it to say that a high-level explanation of "routing" is that it is the process of build-ing the tree, and it occurs when a leaf router initiates a join toward a group's source(s). Routing results in the creation of forwarding state. A router uses this state to look up a group address and determine which outgoing interfaces a multicast packet should be for-warded on.

1.5 Organization of This Book

Understanding the organization of this book is key to knowing what to expect. That is why we describe the book's outline in detail in the Preface and have spent a good part of Chapter 1 describing the pieces. With this in mind, we now present a brief summary of how this book is organized.

The first set of chapters, Chapters 2 through 4, deal with programming multicast sockets in C, Java, and C#. Chapter 5 looks at how the multicast service model is evolving and how this evolution affects the creation of multicast sockets. Chapter 6 looks at key parameters for multicast sockets: the Time-To-Live (TTL) field and the group address. Chapters 7 and 8 discuss advanced topics like scalability, reachability, feedback, and reflectors. Example code is used to demonstrate how these concepts can be applied in practice. Finally, Chapter 9 summarizes the most important lessons to keep in mind when programming multicast sockets.

1.6 Exercises

1. If UDP and TCP are at opposite ends of the spectrum in terms of transport layer services, what services might new transport protocols offer that would be classified somewhere between the two? What applications might be more efficient with these kinds of protocols?

2. What kinds of services might need to broadcast to all hosts on a LAN? List some examples of protocols that exist that currently use LAN-based broadcasts.

3. What kinds of complexity would a TCP-based version of multicast need to handle?

4. How would a TCP-based version of multicast implement the basic TCP services (reliability, congestion control, etc.)?

chapter 2

Multicasting with C Sockets

In the interest of jumping into coding examples as quickly as possible, this chapter introduces the C sockets application programming interface (API) for multicast. Subsequent chapters deal with Java and .NET.

Before getting started with this chapter, you should have a good understanding of exactly what multicast is and know roughly how the protocols work in the Internet to deliver multicast packets. These topics are covered in Chapter 1 and Appendix A. Of course, you should also be familiar with C and have some prior knowledge of socket or network programming [16].

The approach in this chapter is to build out the API and its options through the discussion of simple examples—multicast sender and receiver programs. Additionally, more complicated examples dealing with advanced multicast services are discussed starting in Chapter 5.

2.1 UDP Sockets

Sockets are an application programming interface (API) that provide basic function calls to send data across a network. Originally developed as part of the Berkeley Standard Distribution (BSD) of Unix, sockets have been expanded to be included in almost all Unix variants, Microsoft Windows, MS-DOS, Apple MacOS, OS2, and newer high-level languages such as Java and C# (pronounced "C sharp"). Almost anybody who has done modern network programming is familiar either with the socket API itself or with a higher-level API that utilizes sockets "under the hood."

The most common use of the sockets API is to send a TCP data stream from one host to another. TCP adds important features like connections, multiplexing/demultiplexing, in-order delivery, reliability, and congestion control on top of the IP layer. As discussed in Chapter 1, the one-to-many transmission of multicast packets makes use of TCP and its services impossible.[1] Instead, multicast transmission is integrated into the User Datagram Protocol (UDP). Of the five TCP services listed, UDP provides only multiplexing/demultiplexing. There is no notion of connections, in-order delivery, reliability, or congestion control.

Obviously, UDP is a very basic network protocol. As a result, it has a straightforward API. As an application programmer, you create a logical "socket," which is a handle to the network endpoint from which data can be sent and received. If the goal is to send UDP packets, packets can simply be sent on the socket to a specified host address and port. If the goal is to receive UDP packets, the additional step of "binding" the socket needs to be performed. This step notifies the protocol stack that it should begin forwarding packets destined for that port to the application. Then the application can execute a "read" and wait to begin receiving packets. Unlike TCP, no formal establishment of a connection is required. If the receiver is not listening, the sender will not know and the packets will disappear into the ether. If the sender is not sending, the receiver will wait forever in vain (or at least until the application is terminated, either programmatically or by a frustrated user). If a packet is lost, the receiver may not even be able to detect it. Furthermore, there is no built-in mechanism within the protocol to alert the sender to resend the missing data. Any detection or retransmission of lost packets is strictly up to the application level to deal with.

At first glance, one might assume that these are fatal flaws in the design of UDP. However, this is not the case. For some kinds of applications, UDP is much more appropriate than TCP. For example, consider an application that requires a constant stream of packets and where lost packets do not matter (e.g., streaming audio or video). UDP is well suited because it does not stop and retransmit lost packets. Retransmitted packets are useless because the data will be out of date before it can be re-sent and received. UDP allows application developers to add more lightweight reliability schemes than TCP (e.g., partial reliability for a streamed song). Also, since TCP has all the overhead of establishing and closing connections, UDP can be significantly faster. This is even more important for multicast where the time saved in not having to establish a connection to *every* receiver could be huge. So, in fact, UDP is widely used in streaming applications and for critical Internet protocols such as the Domain Name System (DNS), Network File System (NFS), and Simple Network Management Protocol (SNMP).

In the next two sections, we are going to look at the details of UDP socket calls, and the additional calls and considerations introduced when multicasting packets.

2.2   Sending Multicast Packets in C

We start by examining the four steps required to create a C application that sends multicast packets.

---

[1] As an example of why it is so hard to use multicast with TCP, consider the simple problem of reliability. Where unicast has to keep track of only one receiver, multicast has to keep track of potentially a very large number. In the case where half of a group of millions loses a packet, how should retransmission be handled?

1. Create a socket.

2. Optionally set the scope for the packets.

3. Send the data on the socket.

4. Close the socket.

If you are familiar with unicasting UDP packets, the steps are almost identical for multicast with the exception of setting the scope. Each step is detailed in the following sections.

2.2.1 Socket Creation and Destruction

The first step in sending multicast packets is to create a UDP socket using the C socket() call.

```
#include <sys/types.h>
#include <sys/socket.h>

int socket(int protocolFamily, int type, int protocol);
```

The socket() call creates a socket, which is a handle to the network connection through which data can be sent and received. The socket() call takes three arguments: a protocol family, a protocol type, and a protocol. These three arguments are defined by constant values, which for the purposes of multicasting are almost always the same, as seen in Table 2.1.

- The *protocol family* should be the Internet protocol family, represented by the constant PF_INET.

- The protocol *type* defines the semantics of the protocol. Most network programmers are familiar with TCP's reliable byte stream semantics (SOCK_STREAM). For the purposes of UDP and multicast, best-effort semantics are used (SOCK_DGRAM).

- The Internet *protocol* is most commonly set to TCP (IPPROTO_TCP) or UDP (IPPROTO_UDP). For multicast, this should always be set to IPPROTO_UDP.

The constant values for the arguments are usually defined in the header files sys/socket.h (for the protocol family and type) and netinet/in.h (for the protocol). In most systems, the in.h

Table 2.1 C socket() call arguments.

Argument	Value	Meaning
protocolFamily	PF_INET	Internet protocol family
type	SOCK_DGRAM	Datagram socket
protocol	IPPROTO_UDP	User datagram protocol

header file is automatically included, though on some it may need to be explicitly included; check the local manual pages.

The socket() call returns a positive integer (referred to as the *socket descriptor*) on success or −1 on failure. On failure, errno is set to indicate the error type.

A sample call to create a UDP socket looks like

```
int sock;

if ((sock = socket(PF_INET, SOCK_DGRAM, IPPROTO_UDP)) < 0) {
  /* add error handling here */
}
```

This stores the handle to the socket that has been created in the integer variable sock. If sock is a negative number, some type of error has occurred and needs to be handled.

Finally, when done sending and receiving packets, the socket is closed with the close() call.

```
#include <unistd.h>

int close(int socket);
```

The close() function stops the communication and deallocates the resources for a specified socket descriptor. The close() function returns 0 on success or −1 on failure. On failure, errno is set to indicate the error type.

2.2.2   Specifying Addresses in C

Now that the socket descriptor has been created, the destination address structure needs to be prepared before packets can be sent. For this, a sockaddr data structure needs to be populated with the destination address information.

```
struct sockaddr {
   unsigned short  sa_family;   /* address family */
   char            sa_data[14]; /* up to 14 bytes of addr info */
};
```

The sockaddr structure is defined in the sys/socket.h header and is a generic structure for sockets. To see the details of the sa_data portion of the socket address, look at the data structure sockaddr_in, which is an Internet-specific overlay of the sockaddr data structure. The sockaddr_in structure resides in netinet/in.h. That structure is defined as

```
struct sockaddr_in {
   unsigned short  sin_family;  /* protocol family (AF_INET) */
```

```
    unsigned short  sin_port;    /* 16 bit address port */
    struct  in_addr sin_addr;    /* 32 bit Internet address */
    char            sin_zero[8]; /* unused */
};
```

The family field is set to an Internet address family constant named AF_INET.[2] The port field is set to a network port number. The address field is set to a single host IP address in the case of unicast, or a multicast address for our purposes.

One noteworthy point is that the sin_addr field is actually another structure called in_addr. This is for historical reasons, and simply contains a single unsigned long field that represents the binary value of the IP address.

```
struct in_addr {
    unsigned long s_addr;
};
```

The selection of multicast addresses is very important. Choosing the right address depends on several factors, including the expected scope of the group, the type of multicast service to use, and whether the application is just an experiment or a production tool. Techniques for selecting multicast addresses are described in more detail in Chapter 6.

For the purposes of building a test application, we simplify the address selection problem significantly. To start, multicast addresses are called Class D IP addresses and are in the specific range of 224.0.0.0 to 239.255.255.255. Some of the addresses in this range are reserved for special use. For now, suffice it to say that for simple application-level programming, addresses can be chosen randomly in the 224.2/16 (224.2.0.0 to 224.2.255.255) and 239.255/16 (239.255.0.0 to 239.255.255.255) address ranges. A multicast address is often referred to as a multicast "group" or multicast "channel," further emphasizing the one-to-many paradigm.

As an example, consider choosing the multicast address 239.255.10.10 and port 10000. The address structure would be populated in the following manner:

```
struct sockaddr_in mc_addr;

memset(&mc_addr, 0, sizeof(mc_addr));

mc_addr.sin_family      = AF_INET;
mc_addr.sin_addr.s_addr = inet_addr("239.255.10.10");
mc_addr.sin_port        = htons(10000);
```

The memset() call zeros out the sockaddr_in structure, and the family is set to the AF_INET constant, representing the Internet address family. To properly format the address and port fields, two new functions need to be introduced: inet_addr() and htons().

---

[2]Note that this is a different constant than is used for the protocol family in the socket() call, which is PF_INET, although on most systems these constants resolve to the same value.

```
#include <sys/types.h>
#include <sys/socket.h>
#include <netinet/in.h>
#include <arpa/inet.h>

unsigned long inet_addr(const char *cp);

char *inet_ntoa(const struct in_addr in);
```

The inet_addr() function converts an ASCII text IP address string in dotted quad notation (239.255.10.10) into a long integer. The long integer result is returned in network byte order suitable for populating the sin_addr structure (see the discussion of byte ordering that follows). The inet_addr() call returns −1 if the input argument was malformed and could not be converted to a network address.

The inet_ntoa() function performs the reverse conversion, converting a binary network IP address in the form of an in_addr structure to an ASCII character string in dotted quad notation.

```
#include <sys/types.h>
#include <netinet/in.h>
#include <inttypes.h>

unsigned int htonl(unsigned int hostlong);
unsigned short htons(unsigned short hostshort);
unsigned int ntohl(unsigned int netlong);
unsigned short ntohs(unsigned short netshort);
```

This set of functions is used to ensure that data sent between hosts that process their multibyte binary values differently will still be interpreted properly. This is commonly referred to as the big-endian/little-endian problem. When big-endian machines (Sparc, Motorola 68000, RISC, Mac, IBM 390) read a multibyte binary data type, they consider the leftmost byte to be the most significant (big end first). Little-endian machines (Intel x86, DEC Alpha), however, consider the rightmost byte to be the most significant (little end first). The order used by a local machine is usually referred to as the host order, whereas IP-based networks always use big-endian order (also referred to as network byte order). If numerical data sent over a network has been tranformed by the journey to be a very large value when it should be very small, negative when it should be positive, or vice versa for either, the likely culprit is the little-endian/big-endian conversion problem.

These functions are used to ensure that the binary network fields (IP address, port) are properly interpreted by the network and the binary payload data fields are interpreted to be the same value by the sending and receiving hosts. They are

- htonl(): Host to network long
- htons(): Host to network short

- ntohl(): Network to host long

- ntohs(): Network to host short

On machines where the host order is already big-endian, these functions are typically implemented as no-ops. On hosts where the host order is little-endian, these functions will "flip" the bytes to the desired order. For portability and cross-platform communication, every application programmer should call hton* on their outgoing binary multibyte data and addressing fields, and ntoh* on the incoming binary multibyte data and addressing fields (note that the inet_addr() function call returns the IP address in network order already, so there is no need to call htonl() additionally).

2.2.3   TTL: Setting Multicast Scope

So far we have not discussed anything specific to multicast. In fact, just by populating a multicast address in the sock_addr structure, multicast packets can be sent using just the standard UDP sockets API. However, by default a multicast packet will never be routed off the local subnet unless the Time-To-Live (TTL) is increased.

The TTL field for outgoing multicast traffic is used to control the scope of the multicast packets. TTL is actually a bit of a misnomer since the implementation of TTL is not actually a "time" duration at all, but rather a hop count. When a (multicast-enabled) router receives a multicast packet, it examines the TTL of the packet. If the TTL has a value of 1, it will not be forwarded. If the TTL value is greater than 1, the router will decrement the TTL field in the packet by 1 and forward it appropriately. Therefore, a TTL value of 1 will restrict a multicast packet to the local subnet. If a TTL is not specified, the default is typically set to 1, although this may vary by system and should be checked in the local header definitions. TTL valid values range from 0 to 255 (a value of 0 restricts to the local host). Scoping multicast using a TTL is becoming an outdated mechanism for restricting multicast traffic. The modern version uses different types of Class D addresses to limit the scope. These alternatives are discussed in more detail in Chapter 6.

So how is the TTL set with the C API? TTL is really nothing more than a socket option, so logically it should be set using the standard setsockopt() call.

```
#include <sys/types.h>
#include <sys/socket.h>

int setsockopt(int socket, int level, int optName, void *optVal,
               unsigned int optLen);

int getsockopt(int socket, int level, int optName, const void *optVal,
               unsigned int *optLen)
```

The setsockopt() and getsockopt() calls are used to set and get options, respectively, for a socket. The arguments are the socket descriptor, the level at which the option is applied, the name of the option (as specified by a constant), a pointer to the value of the option (in the case of setsockopt()) or a pointer to where the value of the option should be stored (in the case of getsocktopt()), and the length of the value of the option.

The option level is one of three possibilities:

- SOL_SOCKET: Options that apply at the socket level
- IPPROTO_TCP: Options that apply at the transport (TCP) level
- IPPROTO_IP: Options that apply at the network (IP) level

Every multicast-specific socket option is applied at the IP level (IPPROTO_IP). There are some socket-level options that are useful (but not specific) to multicast that will be discussed later. It is important to note that the level applies to *where* the option is set, not *what* it applies to. All the socket options apply to the socket they are set on only, regardless of level.

Note the subtle difference in the arguments between setsockopt() and getsockopt() since this is a common socket programming mistake. The optVal argument is a pointer to void for setsockopt(), but a *constant* pointer to void for getsockopt(). The optLen argument is an unsigned int for setsockopt(), but a *pointer* to an unsigned int for getsockopt(). Both the setsockopt() and getsockopt() calls return 0 on success and −1 on failure. On failure, errno is set to indicate the error type.

The TTL can be retrieved or set using the IP_MULTICAST_TTL option. The TTL optVal argument is of type unsigned char. This example shows how to retrieve the current TTL setting and set it to a new value.

```
int sock;           /* socket descriptor */
unsigned char ttl;    /* time to live (hop count) */
int ttl_size;

... /* add code to create socket here */

ttl_size = sizeof(ttl);

if ((getsockopt(sock, IPPROTO_IP, IP_MULTICAST_TTL, &ttl, &ttl_size)) < 0) {
  /* add error handling here */
}

printf("Old TTL was %d\n",ttl);

ttl=5; /* set the new ttl value to 5 */

if ((setsockopt(sock, IPPROTO_IP, IP_MULTICAST_TTL, (void*) &ttl, ttl_size)) < 0) {
  /* add error handling here */
}
```

If the intention is to restrict multicast traffic to the local subnet, setting this option is not necessary, but it is good programming practice to do so. Remember, the default may vary from system to system, causing unintended consequences. It is also useful to programmers who may need to read your code in the future to see the intended TTL explicitly stated. It is also a good practice to set the TTL to the lowest functional value that is reasonable. This prevents packet traffic from reaching unintended areas. Though we all hope that the network does the right thing, it never hurts to be careful!

Sometimes two or more multicast-enabled networks are separated by networks that do not support multicast. If an application wants to send and receive multicast traffic between these distant networks, it is common to set up a multicast "tunnel." Tunneled multicast traffic is encapsulated into unicast packets and sent via unicast to a host on the remote multicast-enabled network. Once received by that host, the multicast packets are retrieved from the unicast packets and remulticast out on the remote network. This requires specialized software or hardware on both ends of the network, which will be discussed in more detail in Chapter 8. The important point for TTL is that the software on each end of the tunnel acts like a multicast router as far as decrementing the TTL. That means a single tunneled hop will reduce the TTL by only 2 (once leaving the local subnet, and once being forwarded out on the remote subnet), regardless of the number of unicast-only routers that have been traversed in the tunnel. Some tunneling applications may have a *threshold* value, which is the minimum TTL value a multicast packet can have to be forwarded over the tunnel. Whatever the value of the threshold, each tunneling application will typically still decrement the TTL by a value of only 1 if the packet is forwarded.

2.2.4 Sending Multicast Packets

Once the family, port, and address are populated in the sockaddr structure, the socket is ready to send packets. The sockaddr structure becomes one of the arguments to the sendto() call.

```
#include <sys/types.h>
#include <sys/socket.h>

int sendto(int socket, const void *msg, unsigned int msgLength, int flags,
          struct sockaddr *destAddr, unsigned int addrLen);
```

The sendto() call is used to send a unicast or multicast UDP packet. The arguments are the socket descriptor, a pointer to contents of the packet (the message), the length of the message, any socket flags,[3] a pointer to the address structure of the destination (a single host address for unicast or a multicast address), and the length of the destination address structure. The sendto() call returns the number of bytes sent on success, −1 on failure. On failure, errno is set to indicate the error type.

---

[3] Socket flags are not specific to multicast and are beyond the scope of this book.

2.2.5   Multicast Sender (C Version)

Now that we have covered the APIs and theory, it is time to jump into a code example. The mcsend.c program takes standard input from the keyboard and sends it line by line on the multicast address specified. Control-C quits the program, for example,

```
$ mcsend 239.255.10.10 10000
Begin typing (return to send, ctrl-C to quit):
Sending a test line
^C
```

As a recap, the steps involved in a C multicast sender are as follows:

1. Create a socket using socket().

2. Set the TTL using setsockopt() (optional).

3. Send data using sendto().

4. Close the socket using close().

The following is the full code for a multicast sender:

mcsend.c

```
 1  #include <sys/types.h>    /* for type definitions */
 2  #include <sys/socket.h>   /* for socket API function calls */
 3  #include <netinet/in.h>   /* for address structs */
 4  #include <arpa/inet.h>    /* for sockaddr_in */
 5  #include <stdio.h>        /* for printf() */
 6  #include <stdlib.h>       /* for atoi() */
 7  #include <string.h>       /* for strlen() */
 8  #include <unistd.h>       /* for close() */
 9
10  #define MAX_LEN  1024     /* maximum string size to send */
11  #define MIN_PORT 1024     /* minimum port allowed */
12  #define MAX_PORT 65535    /* maximum port allowed */
13
14  int main(int argc, char *argv[]) {
15
16    int sock;                  /* socket descriptor */
17    char send_str[MAX_LEN];    /* string to send */
18    struct sockaddr_in mc_addr; /* socket address structure */
19    unsigned int send_len;     /* length of string to send */
20    char* mc_addr_str;         /* multicast IP address */
21    unsigned short mc_port;    /* multicast port */
22    unsigned char mc_ttl=1;    /* time to live (hop count) */
23
24    /* validate number of arguments */
25    if (argc != 3) {
26      fprintf(stderr,
```

```
27                 "Usage: %s <Multicast IP> <Multicast Port>\n",
28                 argv[0]);
29       exit(1);
30     }
31
32     mc_addr_str = argv[1];         /* arg 1: multicast IP address */
33     mc_port     = atoi(argv[2]); /* arg 2: multicast port number */
34
35     /* validate the port range */
36     if ((mc_port < MIN_PORT) || (mc_port > MAX_PORT)) {
37       fprintf(stderr, "Invalid port number argument %d.\n",
38               mc_port);
39       fprintf(stderr, "Valid range is between %d and %d.\n",
40               MIN_PORT, MAX_PORT);
41       exit(1);
42     }
43
44     /* create a socket for sending to the multicast address */
45     if ((sock = socket(PF_INET, SOCK_DGRAM, IPPROTO_UDP)) < 0) {
46       perror("socket() failed");
47       exit(1);
48     }
49
50     /* set the TTL (time to live/hop count) for the send */
51     if ((setsockopt(sock, IPPROTO_IP, IP_MULTICAST_TTL,
52         (void*) &mc_ttl, sizeof(mc_ttl))) < 0) {
53       perror("setsockopt() failed");
54       exit(1);
55     }
56
57     /* construct a multicast address structure */
58     memset(&mc_addr, 0, sizeof(mc_addr));
59     mc_addr.sin_family      = AF_INET;
60     mc_addr.sin_addr.s_addr = inet_addr(mc_addr_str);
61     mc_addr.sin_port        = htons(mc_port);
62
63     printf("Begin typing (return to send, ctrl-C to quit):\n");
64
65     /* clear send buffer */
66     memset(send_str, 0, sizeof(send_str));
67
68     while (fgets(send_str, MAX_LEN, stdin)) {
69       send_len = strlen(send_str);
70
71       /* send string to multicast address */
72       if ((sendto(sock, send_str, send_len, 0,
73           (struct sockaddr *) &mc_addr,
74           sizeof(mc_addr))) != send_len) {
75         perror("sendto() sent incorrect number of bytes");
```

```
76        exit(1);
77      }
78
79      /* clear send buffer */
80      memset(send_str, 0, sizeof(send_str));
81    }
82
83    close(sock);
84
85    exit(0);
86  }
```

mcsend.c

Lines 1–8: Include headers for socket programming. The exact include headers for a particular system may vary, so check local system manuals or documentation.

Lines 10–33: Basic variable declaration and argument parsing.

Lines 35–42: Validate that the port input is in the valid range for user applications (1024 to 65535).

Lines 44–48: Create a socket for use with UDP datagrams using the socket() call. For multicast, these arguments will always have the following constant values: the protocol family is PF_INET, the type of protocol is SOCK_DGRAM, and the protocol is IPPROTO_UDP.

Lines 50–55: Set the Time-To-Live (TTL) socket option using the setsockopt() call. The option level is IPPROTO_IP, or the IP layer, and the option name is IP_MULTICAST_TTL. The value argument is a pointer to an integer with the value of the desired TTL. In this program, we set the TTL to 1, assuming the program is being run on the same LAN segment. Since this is also the default on most systems, this call could be omitted entirely, but it is good programming practice to include it. Remember to never set a higher TTL than needed.

Lines 57–61: Populate the address structure, which is no different than with a unicast socket except that the IP address must be in the Class D range (224.0.0.0 to 239.255.255.255). The memset() is used to initialize the entire structure with zeros before the programmer-supplied values are filled in. The sin_family is set to the AF_INET constant, and the sin_address and sin_port are set to the appropriate network byte order multicast address and port values. The inet_addr() function converts a string of an IP address in dotted quad notation into a binary equivalent in network byte order. The htons() function converts the port number into its network byte order equivalent.

Lines 71–77: Send the message using the sendto() call. This is standard unicast UDP socket syntax. If other multicast address structures have been populated, they could be used on subsequent calls to the same socket without modifying anything else.

Line 83: Standard close() call.

2.2.6   Other Multicast Sender Options: Interface and Loopback

The two remaining options for multicast senders are setting the outgoing *interface* and the *loopback*. The IP_MULTICAST_IF option is used to modify the outgoing interface on which multicast packets are sent. This is used on multihomed hosts where the outgoing interface needs to be specified. If an interface on a multihomed host is not specified, the OS will determine the outgoing interface by consulting the routing tables for the multicast address in question. The option value argument for IP_MULTICAST_IF is an in_addr structure containing the IP address of the interface. In most cases, the default interface will be 0.0.0.0, or INADDR_ANY, indicating any outgoing interface. Any attempt to set the interface to an IP address that is not a local interface will fail with a "no route to host" error. Remember that although this is an IP level option, it will apply only to the socket the option is set on. You can have multiple sockets within the same process set different interfaces simultaneously by using multiple IP_MULTICAST_IF setsockopt() calls.

Here is a code example that retrieves and prints the current interface and sets a new interface.

```
int sock;
struct in_addr interface_addr;
int addr_size;

... /* create socket here */

addr_size = sizeof(interface_addr);

/* get the loopback value */
if ((getsockopt(sock, IPPROTO_IP, IP_MULTICAST_IF,
               &interface_addr, &addr_size)) < 0) {
  perror("getsockopt() failed");
  exit(1);
}

printf("The default interface is %s\n", inet_ntoa(interface_addr));

/* note: to run this code on your system, substitute 192.111.52.12
   with a valid local interface or the call will fail */
interface_addr.s_addr = inet_addr("192.111.52.12");

/* set the new default interface */
if ((setsockopt(sock, IPPROTO_IP, IP_MULTICAST_IF,
               &interface_addr, addr_size)) < 0) {
  perror("setsockopt() failed");
  exit(1);
}
```

The loopback of multicast can be toggled on and off using the IP_MULTICAST_LOOP option. When loopback is disabled, a socket that is a member of a multicast group will not receive any packets it sends to the multicast group. The socket's packets are filtered out at the IP layer. Loopback is enabled by default, meaning that a socket will see its own transmission if it joins the group to which it is sending. The option value argument for IP_MULTICAST_LOOP is an unsigned char set to 1 for on or 0 for off.

Here is a simple example that retrieves the value of the multicast loopback option and sets it to the opposite of what it was.

```
int sock;
unsigned char loopback;
int loopback_size;

... /* create socket here */

loopback_size = sizeof(loopback);

/* get the existing loopback value */
if ((getsockopt(sock, IPPROTO_IP, IP_MULTICAST_LOOP,
                &loopback, &loopback_size)) < 0) {
  perror("getsockopt() failed");
  exit(1);
}

if (loopback == 0) {
  printf("Loopback is off\n");
  loopback = 1;
} else {
  printf("Loopback is on\n");
  loopback = 0;
}

/* set the new loopback value */
if ((setsockopt(sock, IPPROTO_IP, IP_MULTICAST_LOOP, &loopback, loopback_size)) < 0) {
  perror("setsockopt() failed");
  exit(1);
}
```

2.3   Receiving Multicast Packets in C

Now that we have described the code to send multicast packets, we will examine the steps involved in receiving multicast packets.

1. Create a socket.

2. Optionally set the port reuse socket option.

3. Bind to the socket.

4. Join the multicast group.

5. Receive multicast data.

6. Drop the multicast group.

7. Close the socket.

Each step is detailed in the following sections.

2.3.1   Socket Creation and Destruction

Just as with sending multicast packets, receiving multicast packets is very much like receiving unicast UDP packets. The first step is to create a socket using the socket() call.

```
int sock;

if ((sock = socket(PF_INET, SOCK_DGRAM, IPPROTO_UDP)) < 0) {
  /* add error handling here */
}
```

Once the socket has been used to receive all packets, a close() call can be issued to deallocate it. The socket() and close() calls are identical to the ones in the multicast sender section, so the definitions will not be repeated here.

2.3.2   Setting the Address Reuse Option

Being able to reuse the same address even if multiple applications bind to that address is a useful function for multicast. The bind itself is discussed in the next section, while setting the reuse option (which must precede the bind) is described here.

On most systems, only one process will be able to bind to a particular port. The second and subsequent processes will typically issue an error on the bind() call (or worse, on some operating systems, even complete the bind call successfully but not receive any packets). In a unicast paradigm, this restriction makes perfect sense. In one-to-one stateful communication, an additional recipient or sender would likely disrupt communication between the intended endpoints. However, with multicast, the paradigm is one to many, and it may be completely valid for multiple processes on the same host to receive the same packets on the same port.

In order to circumvent this issue, one of two socket options (either SO_REUSEPORT or SO_REUSEADDR) can be set to indicate that more than one bind is allowed to the same socket. Unlike our earlier socket options, both these options are set at the socket level (SOL_SOCKET). In order for the reuse options to work, every process running simultaneously on a given host that attempts to bind on the specified port must set one of these options prior to making their bind() call.

The following is a simple example that sets the socket option to allow a socket to be reused:

```
int sock;      /* socket descriptor */
int flag = 1;  /* turn flag on */

... /* create socket here */

if ((setsockopt(sock, SOL_SOCKET, SO_REUSEPORT, &flag, sizeof(flag))) < 0) {
  /* add error handling here */
}
```

Not all systems support SO_REUSEPORT, which was created specifically for multicast. For those that do not, SO_REUSEADDR can usually be used to the same effect.

Note that setting the address reuse option is optional. If allowing more than one receiver on a single host to use a socket is not required, it can be omitted.

2.3.3   Binding an Address to a Socket

An additional step required to receive packets is a bind.

```
#include <sys/types.h>
#include <sys/socket.h>

int bind(int socket, struct sockaddr *localAddress, unsigned int addressLength);
```

The bind() call is used with UDP sockets when datagrams are expected to be received by the socket. The bind() call triggers the protocol stack to begin passing packets to the application on the requested address and port. The arguments are the socket descriptor, a pointer to the address structure, and the length of the address structure. The address structure is the standard sockaddr / sockaddr_in structure discussed earlier.

```
struct sockaddr_in {
    unsigned short  sin_family;  /* protocol family (AF_INET) */
    unsigned short  sin_port;    /* 16 bit address port */
    struct  in_addr sin_addr;    /* 32 bit Internet address */
    char            sin_zero[8]; /* unused */
};
```

It is important to remember that failure of all processes on a single host to set the address or port reuse option before calling bind() may result in bind failures or runtime failures, as discussed in the prior section. bind() returns 0 on success and −1 on failure. On failure, errno is set to indicate the error type.

2.3.4   Adding Multicast Membership

Once the bind is complete, a multicast-specific call needs to be performed in order to begin receiving multicast packets. We mentioned earlier that multicast addresses are often referred to as a multicast group. In order to receive packets for a specific multicast group, a host needs to announce its intention to add membership for that group. When a host wants to stop receiving packets, it needs to drop membership in the multicast group. These announcements are sent via the C sockets API using setsockopt().[4]

An add membership is requested with the socket option IP_ADD_MEMBERSHIP. As for all other multicast-specific socket options, the option level is IP_PROTO. When a host makes an add membership request, two things happen. First, the IP stack begins to pass packets heard

---

[4] Group membership is not exactly a socket option, but this is a case where the existing API was overloaded to achieve the desired functionality.

on that multicast group up to the transport layer (UDP in this case) and on to the application. Second, an Internet Group Management Protocol (IGMP) message is sent to the router(s) on the local subnet indicating the host would like to receive packets on that particular multicast address. If the router(s) on the local subnet are multicast enabled and are connected to other networks that are also multicast enabled, the IGMP join message will be transformed into a multicast routing protocol join and will be propagated through the network. The result is the formation of a branch from the group's multicast tree to the local network. Any sources sending on the particular multicast address will then reach the receiving application—assuming that the TTL is sufficient to cover the router hops from the source to the receiver. More details on how routing occurs and how the forwarding tree is formed and maintained can be found in Appendix A.

The same socket can listen on multiple multicast addresses at the same time. Simply adding additional setsockopt() calls to IP_ADD_MEMBERSHIP with different multicast addresses will work cumulatively, allowing the socket to receive packets intended for any of the specified addresses. An upper bound is usually applied by the operating system, and although it varies by system it is commonly set to 20. If there is a need for an additional number of joins, it can be achieved at the application layer by using multiple sockets.

The option that is passed to the setsockopt() call is a structure called ip_mreq. That structure consists of two address structures.

```
struct ip_mreq {
    struct in_addr imr_multiaddr; /* Group multicast address */
    struct in_addr imr_interface; /* Local interface address */
}
```

The imr_multiaddr field is simply set to the network IP address of the multicast group you want to join or drop. The imr_interface field is set to the network interface you want to receive packets on. If you are using a multihomed host, you can specifically set it; otherwise, it can be set to INADDR_ANY, meaning any incoming interface.

Here is a sample join.

```
int sock;
struct ip_mreq mc_req;

... /* create and bind socket here */

/* construct an IGMP join request structure */
mc_req.imr_multiaddr.s_addr = inet_addr("239.255.10.10");
mc_req.imr_interface.s_addr = htonl(INADDR_ANY);

/* send an ADD MEMBERSHIP message via setsockopt */
if ((setsockopt(sock, IPPROTO_IP, IP_ADD_MEMBERSHIP,
                (void*) &mc_req, sizeof(mc_req))) < 0) {
  perror("setsockopt() failed");
  exit(1);
}
```

Note that, unlike with the other multicast socket options, there is no `getsockopt()` for added or dropped memberships.

2.3.5 Receiving Multicast Packets

Once a socket has been created and bound (with address reuse optionally set), and multicast membership added, it is ready to receive multicast packets. Multicast packets are received using the same call as unicast UDP packets, with the `recvfrom()` call.

```
#include <sys/types.h>
#include <sys/socket.h>

int recvfrom(int socket, const void *msg, unsigned int msgLength, int flags,
             struct sockaddr *srcAddr, unsigned int addrLen);
```

The `recvfrom()` call is used to receive a unicast or multicast UDP packet. The arguments are the socket descriptor, a pointer to a buffer where the contents of the packet (message) can be stored, the maximum size of the buffer, any socket flags,[5] a pointer to an address structure that will be populated with the source address that the packet was received from, and a reference to the length of the source address structure. By default, `recvfrom()` is a blocking call, meaning `recvfrom()` will not return until packets are received or it is interrupted in some manner. The `recvfrom()` call returns the number of bytes received on success, −1 on failure. On failure, errno is set to indicate the error type.

2.3.6 Dropping Multicast Membership

Once an application no longer wishes to receive packets on a particular multicast address, a call to `setsockopt()` with `IP_DROP_MEMBERSHIP` will cause the IP stack to stop forwarding packets received on that multicast address to the application. If that application is the only application on the host to be requesting the traffic on that address, this will also generate an IGMP *leave* message from the host to the subnet's router(s). If the host is the last host requesting membership of that multicast group on the subnet, the Internet forwarding tree will be modified to "prune" the connecting branches. Packets will stop being forwarded to the particular subnet. Closing a socket or terminating a program with multicast membership will also generate a drop request automatically, so an explicit `IP_DROP_MEMBERSHIP` is not necessarily required. However, as with explicit closes to sockets and file descriptors, it is good practice to always include them.

Sample code for dropping a multicast membership is identical to our earlier add membership example, with the exception that the option name is `IP_DROP_MEMBERSHIP`.

---

[5] Socket flags are not specific to multicast and are beyond the scope of this book.

2.3.7 Multicast Receiver (C Version)

We will now present a multicast receiver program. As a recap, the steps involved in a C multicast receiver are as follows:

1. Create a socket using the socket() call.

2. Call setsockopt() to allow port reuse (SOL_REUSEPORT or SOL_REUSEADDR—optional).

3. Bind to the socket using the bind() call.

4. Join the multicast group using an IGMP IP_ADD_MEMBERSHIP setsockopt() call.

5. Receive data using recvfrom().

6. Drop the multicast group using an IGMP IP_DROP_MEMBERSHIP setsockopt() call (optional).

7. Close the socket using close().

The following is the full code for a multicast receiver:

mcreceive.c

```
 1  #include <sys/types.h>  /* for type definitions */
 2  #include <sys/socket.h> /* for socket API calls */
 3  #include <netinet/in.h> /* for address structs */
 4  #include <arpa/inet.h>  /* for sockaddr_in */
 5  #include <stdio.h>      /* for printf() and fprintf() */
 6  #include <stdlib.h>     /* for atoi() */
 7  #include <string.h>     /* for strlen() */
 8  #include <unistd.h>     /* for close() */
 9
10  #define MAX_LEN  1024   /* maximum receive string size */
11  #define MIN_PORT 1024   /* minimum port allowed */
12  #define MAX_PORT 65535  /* maximum port allowed */
13
14  int main(int argc, char *argv[]) {
15
16    int sock;                 /* socket descriptor */
17    int flag_on = 1;          /* socket option flag */
18    struct sockaddr_in mc_addr;  /* socket address structure */
19    char recv_str[MAX_LEN+1];    /* buffer to receive string */
20    int recv_len;             /* length of string received */
21    struct ip_mreq mc_req;    /* multicast request structure */
22    char* mc_addr_str;        /* multicast IP address */
23    unsigned short mc_port;   /* multicast port */
24    struct sockaddr_in from_addr; /* packet source */
25    unsigned int from_len;    /* source addr length */
26
27    /* validate number of arguments */
28    if (argc != 3) {
```

```
29      fprintf(stderr,
30              "Usage: %s <Multicast IP> <Multicast Port>\n",
31              argv[0]);
32      exit(1);
33    }
34
35    mc_addr_str = argv[1];      /* arg 1: multicast ip address */
36    mc_port = atoi(argv[2]);    /* arg 2: multicast port number */
37
38    /* validate the port range */
39    if ((mc_port < MIN_PORT) || (mc_port > MAX_PORT)) {
40      fprintf(stderr, "Invalid port number argument %d.\n",
41              mc_port);
42      fprintf(stderr, "Valid range is between %d and %d.\n",
43              MIN_PORT, MAX_PORT);
44      exit(1);
45    }
46
47    /* create socket to join multicast group on */
48    if ((sock = socket(PF_INET, SOCK_DGRAM, IPPROTO_UDP)) < 0) {
49      perror("socket() failed");
50      exit(1);
51    }
52
53    /* set reuse port to on to allow multiple binds per host */
54    if ((setsockopt(sock, SOL_SOCKET, SO_REUSEADDR, &flag_on,
55          sizeof(flag_on))) < 0) {
56      perror("setsockopt() failed");
57      exit(1);
58    }
59
60    /* construct a multicast address structure */
61    memset(&mc_addr, 0, sizeof(mc_addr));
62    mc_addr.sin_family      = AF_INET;
63    mc_addr.sin_addr.s_addr = htonl(INADDR_ANY);
64    mc_addr.sin_port        = htons(mc_port);
65
66    /* bind multicast address to socket */
67    if ((bind(sock, (struct sockaddr *) &mc_addr,
68          sizeof(mc_addr))) < 0) {
69      perror("bind() failed");
70      exit(1);
71    }
72
73    /* construct an IGMP join request structure */
74    mc_req.imr_multiaddr.s_addr = inet_addr(mc_addr_str);
75    mc_req.imr_interface.s_addr = htonl(INADDR_ANY);
```

```
76
77    /* send an ADD MEMBERSHIP message via setsockopt */
78    if ((setsockopt(sock, IPPROTO_IP, IP_ADD_MEMBERSHIP,
79        (void*) &mc_req, sizeof(mc_req))) < 0) {
80      perror("setsockopt() failed");
81      exit(1);
82    }
83
84    for (;;) {            /* loop forever */
85
86      /* clear the receive buffers & structs */
87      memset(recv_str, 0, sizeof(recv_str));
88      from_len = sizeof(from_addr);
89      memset(&from_addr, 0, from_len);
90
91      /* block waiting to receive a packet */
92      if ((recv_len = recvfrom(sock, recv_str, MAX_LEN, 0,
93          (struct sockaddr*)&from_addr, &from_len)) < 0) {
94        perror("recvfrom() failed");
95        exit(1);
96      }
97
98      /* output received string */
99      printf("Received %d bytes from %s: ", recv_len,
100             inet_ntoa(from_addr.sin_addr));
101      printf("%s", recv_str);
102    }
103
104    /* send a DROP MEMBERSHIP message via setsockopt */
105    if ((setsockopt(sock, IPPROTO_IP, IP_DROP_MEMBERSHIP,
106        (void*) &mc_req, sizeof(mc_req))) < 0) {
107      perror("setsockopt() failed");
108      exit(1);
109    }
110
111    close(sock);
112  }
```

mcreceive.c

Lines 1–8: Include headers for socket programming. The exact include headers for a system may vary; check the local system manuals.

Lines 10–36: Basic variable declaration and argument parsing.

Lines 38–45: Validate that the port input is in the valid range for user applications (1024 to 65535).

Lines 47–51: Create a socket for use with UDP datagrams with the socket() call. The standard constants for UDP and multicast are used. The protocol family is PF_INET, the protocol type is SOCK_DGRAM, and the protocol is IPPROTO_UDP.

Lines 53–58: Set reuse address socket option to "on" using the setsockopt() call. This will allow multiple processes on the same host to join the multicast group.

Lines 60–64: Populate the address structure. The memset() function is used to populate the entire structure with zeros before the programmer-supplied values are inserted. The sin_family is set to the AF_INET constant, and the sin_address and sin_port are set to the appropriate network byte order multicast address and port values. The inet_addr() function converts a string of an IP address in dotted quad notation into a binary equivalent in network byte order. The htons() function converts the port number into its network byte order equivalent.

Lines 66–71: Bind to the multicast address using the bind() call. This will fail if another process on the same host has already bound to this address and did not set the SO_REUSEADDR or the SO_REUSEPORT option.

Lines 73–75: Populate the ip_mreq multicast address structure. The ip_mreq structure is populated in preparation for the setsockopt() call. The imr_multiaddr multicast address field is populated with the multicast group address to be joined, and the imr_interface interface field is set to the interface on which to receive. The interface is typically set to INADDR_ANY, specifying any inbound interface, although it could be set to an IP address for a multihomed host. The inet_addr() function converts a string of an IP address in dotted quad notation into a binary equivalent. The htonl() function converts the interface number into its network byte order equivalent.

Lines 77–82: Send the IP_ADD_MEMBERSHIP request. Using the populated ip_mreq structure, the setsockopt() call to join the multicast group is made. The arguments are the socket descriptor, the option level (IPPROTO_IP), the request type (IP_ADD_MEMBERSHIP), a reference to the ip_mreq structure, and the length of the ip_mreq structure.

Lines 91–96: Block waiting for packets to arrive with the recvfrom() call.

Lines 98–101: Output the results of the received packet.

Lines 104–109: Send a DROP_MEMBERSHIP message via setsockopt(). In this particular case, the explicit drop of the multicast membership is not required because it is immediately followed by a socket close() call, which implicitly drops any group memberships. It is good practice to include this explicitly.

Line 111: Close the socket with the close() call.

2.4   A Sample Run of Sender and Receiver(s)

The mcsend application takes the multicast address and port to send to as arguments. Everything typed on the command line is transmitted on that multicast address until Control-C is used to terminate the program.

```
% mcsend 239.255.10.10 9000
Begin typing (return to send, Control-C to quit):
```

```
Testing123
Testing321
^C
```

The mcreceive application takes the multicast address and port to listen on as arguments. The program then receives and echos to the terminal any packets received on that multicast address, until terminated by hitting Control-C.

```
% mcreceive 224.255.10.10 9000
Received 10 bytes from 192.111.52.12: Testing123
Received 10 bytes from 192.111.52.12: Testing321
^C
```

Regardless of the number of receivers run, all the receivers should receive the exact same results (as long as they all have multicast connectivity to the sender and are within the TTL scope). As an initial test, you can run a copy of the sender and receiver on the same host. Then you can expand to different hosts on the same subnet, and, if you are on a multicast-enabled network, to other subnets as well. Once you have the sender and receiver programs working, see the questions at the end of the chapter for some modifications to try out.

2.5   C and Source Specific Multicast

So far, we have discussed the C sockets API for Any Source Multicast (ASM). A more recent development in multicast is called Source Specific Multicast (SSM), which adds additional functionality into multicast. Two new overloaded socket option calls are associated with SSM. Since SSM is a relatively new development and not yet widely implemented, the SSM-specific C sockets API will be discussed separately in Chapter 5.

2.6   Winsock Modifications

Microsoft's version of sockets for Windows is called Winsock and has some minor differences in the libraries, headers, and syntax from what we have presented in this chapter. We have included a list of changes needed to make the programs in this chapter compile using Winsock. Microsoft's new .NET framework appears to be supplanting the direct API, however, and the .NET sockets interface is described in more detail in Chapter 4, along with examples in C#.

The changes to mcsend.c and mcreceive.c required for Winsock are

1. **Header changes:** The include lines for sys/socket.h and arpa/inet.h should be replaced with winsock.h.

2. **Link changes:** The ws2_32.lib library file will need to be linked with the executables. In Visual C++ Studio, this can be done by adding it to the *Project Settings* window in the *Link* tab in the *Object/library modules* field.

3. **Library load changes:** The Winsock DLL (dynamic load library) needs to be explicitly loaded before it can be used. Prior to calling any of the socket APIs, the following code will need to be inserted in order to load the DLL:

```
WSADATA wsaData;

/* Load Winsock 2.0 DLL */
if (WSAStartup(MAKEWORD(2, 0), &wsaData) != 0) {
  fprintf(stderr, "WSAStartup() failed");
  exit(1);
}
```

In this case, MAKEWORD(2, 0) indicates that the application is requesting the loading of Winsock version 2.0. If an older version of Winsock is needed, such as 1.1, MAKEWORD(1, 1) should be used instead.[6]

4. **Prototype changes:** The prototype for the sendto() function for Winsock takes an integer as the msgLength and addrLen arguments, instead of an unsigned integer.

```
int sendto(int socket, const void *msg, int msgLength, int flags,
          struct sockaddr *destAddr, int addrLen)
```

This means in mcsender.c the strLength variable needs to either be changed from an unsigned int to an int, or be cast to an int in the sendto() function call.

Winsock versions of mcsend.c and mcreceive.c with a makefile are available on the book's Web site at *www.mkp.com/practical/multicast/*.

2.7 Exercises

1. Modify the multicast receiver code to not reuse the ports prior to the bind() call. Now attempt to run multiple copies of the program. What errors do you get?

2. Change the multicast receiver to listen on multiple multicast addresses and ports simultaneously. Verify that it can receive packets on both by running multiple senders on the different addresses.

3. A standard unicast server can easily log its clients, but a multicast sender cannot. Can you think of any mechanisms that would allow a multicast sender to do this? What sort of scalability issues would those mechanisms have?

4. Try combining the multicast sender and receiver into a single program. How can you handle simultaneous sending and receiving? (Hint: You will want to either fork a new process or use multithreading.)

---

[6] If an older version of Winsock is being used, there will be differences in the header and library files as well. Check your system documentation.

chapter **3**

Multicasting with Java

This chapter will introduce the basic classes and methods for sending multicast datagrams in the Java programming language. Java is a cross-platform language introduced by Sun Microsystems, and its basic networking API derives from C sockets. In fact, on most systems, Java byte code interpreters and compilers are written in C and utilize C sockets under the hood. If you have familiarized yourself with the C socket API, you are going to notice a lot in common.

The approach of this chapter will be the same as the chapter on C sockets. We will introduce the Java sockets API through a discussion of building a simple multicast sender and receiver program. Then we will show the annotated code for both programs.

3.1   The Java MulticastSocket API

Java provides a multicast-specific subclass of DatagramSocket called MulticastSocket. The MulticastSocket class allows access to generic socket methods available in DatagramSocket, while allowing the overriding of existing methods and creation of new methods for specialized multicast functionality.

Unless stated otherwise, all the classes described in the chapter belong to the java.net package. An application will need to explicitly import the java.net package at the beginning of the code.

```
import java.net.*;
```

Several Java multicast classes and methods introduced in this book are Java version dependent. To determine which version of Java is installed, the –version option of the java command can be used.

```
$ java -version
java version "1.4.0"
Java(TM) 2 Runtime Environment, Standard Edition (build 1.4.0-b92)
Java HotSpot(TM) Client VM (build 1.4.0-b92, mixed mode)
```

Unfortunately, Java does not provide a good method for determining the version number during runtime, but a free upgrade to the latest version is available on Sun's Java Web site at *java.sun.com*.

3.2   A Java Multicast Sender

We now examine the steps required to create a Java application to send multicast packets.

1. Create a socket.

2. Optionally set the scope for the packets.

3. Send the data on the socket.

4. Close the socket.

Each step is detailed in the following sections.

3.2.1   Socket Creation and Destruction

The first step is to create a socket, or handle, to the network endpoint from which data can be sent and received. In Java, a multicast socket is created by creating an instance of the MulticastSocket class.

```
public java.net.MulticastSocket throws IOException
```

Constructors:

```
MulticastSocket();
MulticastSocket(int port);
MulticastSocket(SocketAddress bindaddr); (New in Java 2 v1.4:)
```

The MulticastSocket constructor call is used to create a socket, which is the handle to a network endpoint for sending and receiving multicast data. The constructor can take optional arguments of a port or a SocketAddress class in which to bind. However, these options are discussed in the next section on receiving multicast packets. For the purposes of sending, there is no need to use any arguments at all. A call to create a MulticastSocket instance can be as simple as

```
try {
  MulticastSocket ms = new MulticastSocket();
} catch (IOException ioe) {
  /* add error handling here */
}
```

Once an application is done with a socket, it should close it so any resources can be reclaimed by the system. This is done with the MulticastSocket method close().

MulticastSocket method:

```
public void close()
```

MulticastSocket throws an IOException on error.

3.2.2 Specifying Addresses in Java

Now that we have seen how a MulticastSocket is created, the next step is to focus on how to create an address structure. In Java, the most common address structure is the InetAddress class.

```
public class java.net.InetAddress extends Object implements Serializable
```

Selected Methods:

```
public static InetAddress getByName(String host) throws UnknownHostException
public String getHostAddress()
public boolean isMulticastAddress()
```

There are several ways to create an instance of the InetAddress class, but using the getByName() method is one of the most common. This method takes an IP address (or hostname) in string form and converts it into an InetAddress class instance. If the IP or hostname argument is invalid or cannot be found, the call will throw an UnknownHostException, which can be caught and processed appropriately. Here is a simple example.

```
try {
  InetAddress mcAddress = InetAddress.getByName("239.255.10.10");
} catch (UnknownHostException e) {
  // add exception handling here
}
```

The InetAddress class also has an isMulticastAddress() method to determine if a given address is a multicast address. Once the InetAddress class has successfully been instantiated, the isMulticastAddress() method can be called to determine if the address is a Class D address or not.[1]

```
if (mcAddress.isMulticastAddress()) {
    System.out.println(InetAddress.getHostAddress() +
                    "is a valid multicast address\n");
```

[1] Beginning in Java 2 v1.4, there are also several other InetAddress methods that can be used to determine exactly what subtype a multicast address is, but that will be discussed in more detail in Chapter 6.

```
    } else {
        System.out.println(InetAddress.getHostAddress() +
                            "is not a valid multicast address\n");
    }
```

The getHostAddress() method in this example is used to return the IP address as a string in standard dotted quad notation.

3.2.3   Populating a Java Multicast Packet

Java uses an object-oriented programming methodology, and part of this approach is storing all the data associated with an object in the instance of that object itself. What this means for datagram packets is that the addressing information of a packet is actually stored in a DatagramPacket class instance along with the packet's data.

This also has the side effect that neither a particular address nor a port needs to be associated with a MulticastSocket instance. In fact, the default constructor for MulticastSocket does not need to take any arguments. A MulticastSocket can be created and then used to send ten packets to that socket, all with different destinations. The following is an example of how to populate a DatagramPacket.

```
public final class java.net.DatagramPacket extends Object
```

Selected Constructors:

```
DatagramPacket(byte[] buf, int length, InetAddress address, int port)
DatagramPacket(byte[] buf, int offset, int length, InetAddress address, int port)
```

There are more DatagramPacket constructors, but we are going to primarily use these two for creating new multicast packets. The constructor arguments are a byte array of the data to be sent, an optional offset from the beginning of the data, the length of the data, the IP address to be sent to in the form of an InetAddress class, and a port. A sample call to DatagramPacket might look like

```
byte[]        sendBytes = "Hello World";
InetAddress   mcAddress = InetAddress.getByName("239.255.10.10");
int           mcPort    = 10000;

DatagramPacket packet = new DatagramPacket(sendBytes,
                                           sendBytes.length,
                                           mcAddress, mcPort);
```

The DatagramPacket instance of the packet now contains both the data to send ("Hello World") and the multicast address and port for where the data is to be sent.

3.2.4 TTL: Setting the Multicast Scope

The Time-To-Live (TTL) determines the number of multicast-enabled router hops a sent packet will be able to traverse before it is discarded. For a more detailed description of how TTL works, see Section 2.2.3. Here, we demonstrate how to get and set the TTL for a given multicast socket in Java.

MulticastSocket methods (Java 2 v1.2 or higher):

```
public void setTimeToLive(int ttl) throws IOException
public int getTimeToLive() throws IOException
```

MulticastSocket methods (Java 2 v1.1 or earlier):

```
public void setTTL(byte ttl) throws IOException
public byte getTTL() throws IOException
```

The default TTL, if left unspecified, is always 1. If the TTL is not in the range of 0 to 255, an IllegalArgumentException will be thrown.

The getTTL() and setTTL() calls are deprecated and relevant only if Java 2 v1.1 or earlier is being used.

3.2.5 Sending Multicast Packets

Once the MulticastSocket has been created and the DatagramPacket is populated, packets can be sent. The transmission of packets is achieved through the send() method of the MulticastSocket class.

MulticastSocket method:

```
public void send(DatagramPacket p) throws IOException
```

MulticastClass method (deprecated in Java 2 v1.4 and later):

```
public void send(DatagramPacket p, byte ttl) throws IOException
```

The single argument of the send() method is the packet to be sent. Remember that the addressing information is contained within the packet class itself. The send() call throws an IOException on error.

In versions prior to Java 2 v1.4, an optional argument was the TTL, which would override any socket-level TTL specified. Overriding the TTL in the send() method has been deprecated as of Java 2 v1.4.

3.2.6 Multicast Sender (Java Version)

We now present a complete Java multicast sender example. Just like the C version from the previous chapter, the mcsend.java program takes standard input from the keyboard and sends it line by line on the multicast address specified. Control-C quits the program. As a recap, the steps involved in a Java multicast sender are as follows:

1. Construct an instance of MulticastSocket.

2. Set the TTL using the setTimeToLive() method (optional).

3. Send data using the send() method.

4. Close the socket using the close() method.

mcsend.java

```
1   import java.net.*;   /* import networking package */
2   import java.io.*;    /* import input/output package */
3
4   public class mcsend {
5
6     public static final int MIN_PORT = 1024;  /* min network port */
7     public static final int MAX_PORT = 65535; /* max network port */
8
9     public static void main(String argv[]) {
10
11      InetAddress mcAddress=null;  /* multicast address */
12      int mcPort=0;                /* multicast port */
13      int ttl=1;                   /* time to live */
14      BufferedReader stdin;        /* input from keyboard */
15      String sendString;           /* string to be sent */
16      byte[] sendBytes;            /* bytes to be sent */
17
18      /* validate number of arguments */
19      if (argv.length != 2) {
20        System.out.println("Usage: mcsend " +
21                           "<Multicast IP> <Multicast Port>");
22        System.exit(1);
23      }
24
25      /* validate the multicast address argument */
26      try {
27        mcAddress = InetAddress.getByName(argv[0]);
28      } catch (UnknownHostException e) {
29        System.err.println(argv[0] + " is not a valid IP address");
30        System.exit(1);
31      }
32
```

```
33      /* validate address argument is a multicast IP */
34      if (! mcAddress.isMulticastAddress()) {
35        System.err.println(mcAddress.getHostAddress() +
36                              " is not a multicast IP address.");
37        System.exit(1);
38      }
39
40      /* parse and validate port argument */
41      try {
42        mcPort = Integer.parseInt(argv[1]);
43      } catch (NumberFormatException nfe) {
44        System.err.println("Invalid port number (" + argv[1] + ")");
45        System.exit(1);
46      }
47
48      if ((mcPort < MIN_PORT) || (mcPort > MAX_PORT)) {
49        System.out.println("Invalid port number " + mcPort);
50        System.out.println("Port should be in range " + MIN_PORT
51                              + " to " + MAX_PORT);
52        System.exit(1);
53      }
54
55      try {
56
57        /* instantiate a MulticastSocket */
58        MulticastSocket sock = new MulticastSocket();
59
60        /* set the time to live */
61        sock.setTimeToLive(ttl); // Java 1.0/1.1 use setTTL()
62
63        /* prepare to read from the keyboard input */
64        stdin=new BufferedReader(new InputStreamReader(System.in));
65
66        System.out.println("Begin typing (return to send," +
67                              " ctrl-C to quit):");
68
69        while ((sendString=stdin.readLine()) != null) {
70
71          /* convert keyboard input to bytes */
72          sendBytes=sendString.getBytes();
73
74          /* populate the DatagramPacket */
75          DatagramPacket packet = new DatagramPacket(sendBytes, sendBytes.length,
76                                                      mcAddress, mcPort);
77
78          /* send the packet */
79          sock.send(packet);
```

```
80          }
81          sock.close();
82
83       } catch (IOException e) {
84          System.err.println(e.toString());
85          System.exit(1);
86       }
87    }
88 }
```

mcsend.java

Lines 1–2: Import the java.net and java.io packages for the networking and IO classes.

Lines 6–23: Standard variable declaration and argument validation.

Lines 25–31: Use InetAddress method getByName() to create an InetAddress instance of the requested IP address. If the input is not a valid IP address, catch the UnknownHostException.

Lines 33–38: Use the InetAddress method isMulticastAddress() to ensure the IP argument is in the correct range for multicast.

Lines 40–53: Parse the port argument and throw an error if it's invalid. Verify the port is in the valid range for user applications (1024 to 65535).

Lines 57–58: Create a new MulticastSocket. Catch the IOException in case of an error.

Lines 60–61: Set the TTL for the socket using the MulticastSocket method setTimeToLive(). If the default of 1 is the desired TTL, this call can be omitted. Remember that in Java 1.1 this call should be setTTL(byte ttl) instead. Catch an IOException in case of error.

Lines 63–64: Set up a BufferedReader class to read lines from the keyboard.

Lines 71–72: Convert the string data to bytes for population in the packet.

Lines 74–76: Create a new DatagramPacket with the payload in bytes, the payload length, the multicast address, and the multicast port. Catch the IOException in case of error.

Lines 78–79: Send the packet using the MulticastSocket method send(). Catch the IOException in case of error.

Line 81: Closes the socket using the MulticastSocket method close().

Lines 83–86: Catch any errors that may occur while populating and sending packets. Note that in this example we used one catch block for several method calls. If you wanted to catch individual errors and perform different actions for each, these could be separated into multiple try/catch blocks.

3.2.7 Other Multicast Sender Options: Interface and Loopback

Multihomed multicast senders can opt to choose the interface on which they send their multicast packets. Multicast senders can also choose whether they want multicast packets they send to be looped back to the local host. These options are set by specific MulticastSocket methods.

MulticastSocket methods:

```
public InetAddress getInterface() throws SocketException
public void setInterface(InetAddress inf) throws SocketException
```

MulticastSocket methods (Java 2 v1.4 and higher):

```
public NetworkInterface getNetworkInterface() throws SocketException
public void setNetworkInterface(NetworkInterface NetIf) throws
                                                   SocketException
```

The getInterface() and setInterface() methods allow the outgoing interface for multi-cast packets to be retrieved and set. The argument to setInterface() and the return value for getInterface() are both an InetAddress instance. Beginning in Java 1.4, new methods getNetworkInterface() and setNetworkInterface() were introduced. They work identically to the other method except that they use the new NetworkInterface class instead of the InetAddress class. All the calls throw a SocketException on error.

The NetworkInterface class will also be important later on, and we define it here.

```
public final class NetworkInterface extends Object (New in Java 2 v1.4)
```

Selected Methods:

```
public static NetworkInterface getByName(String name)
                                      throws SocketException
public static NetworkInterface getByInetAddress(InetAddress addr)
                                      throws SocketException
```

The NetworkInterface class, new in Java 2 v1.4, is a class that specifically defines a network interface object. In versions of Java prior to 1.4, the InetAddress class would double as a network interface class when required. A NetworkInterface instance can be returned by calling either the getByName() method or the getByInetAddress() method using the argument of the IP address string or an InetAddress instance, respectively.

Assuming a MulticastSocket has already been created, here is sample code that gets and sets the multicast sending interface.

```
try {
  InetAddress interface = sock.getInterface();
  System.out.println("Current interface is "
                  + interface.getHostAddress());

  // use the getLocalHost() method to retrieve the host's IP
  interface = InetAddress.getLocalHost();
```

```
    sock.setInterface(interface);
    System.out.println("New interface is "
                        + interface.getHostAddress());
} catch (IOException e) {
    // add error handling here
}
```

MulticastSocket methods (Java 2 v1.4 and higher):

```
public boolean getLoopbackMode() throws SocketException
public void setLoopbackMode(boolean disable) throws SocketException
```

The getLoopbackMode() and setLoopbackMode() methods can be used to get and set the loopback mode, which determines whether sent multicast packets are looped back to the sending host. These methods have become available only in Java 2 v1.4 and higher. There was no mechanism to set this in prior versions, which defaulted to loopback being on. The Java documentation indicates that this call is only a "hint" to the underlying operating system and is not guaranteed to have the desired result. The argument to setLoopbackMode() and the return value for getLoopbackMode() are both a boolean value. A boolean value of false indicates the loopback is disabled; a boolean value of true indicates the loopback is enabled. The default is true (enabled). Both calls throw a SocketException on error.

Here is sample code that gets the loopback value and toggles it to the opposite value.

```
try {
    boolean loopback = s.getLoopbackMode();

    System.out.println("The default loopback is set to "
                        + loopback);

    s.setLoopbackMode(!loopback);

    System.out.println("The new loopback is set to "
                        + s.getLoopbackMode());
} catch (IOException e) {
    // add error handling here
}
```

3.3   Receiving Multicast Packets in Java

Now that we have described the code to send multicast packets, we will examine the steps involved in receiving multicast packets.

1. Create a socket.

2. Optionally set the port reuse socket option.

3. Join the multicast group.

4. Receive multicast data.

5. Drop the multicast group.

6. Close the socket.

Each step is detailed in the following sections.

3.3.1 Socket Creation and Destruction

Using Java to receive multicast packets starts with the creation of an instance of the MulticastSocket class. This is the same class that the multicast sender uses, except now the constructor with a port argument is used.

```
try {
  MulticastSocket sock=new MulticastSocket(10000);
} catch (IOException ioe) {
  // add exception handling here
}
```

The definition of the MulticastSocket class is identical to the sender section and is not repeated here.

3.3.2 Setting the Address Reuse Option

Once a MulticastSocket has been created, the address reuse socket option needs to be set if the ability to create multiple listening sockets on the same port and host is needed. See Section 2.3.2 for more details.

This option is new in Java 2 v1.4 and was always set to true by default in all earlier versions. If you are porting multicast code from Java 2 v1.3 or earlier to a newer version, keep in mind that this option must now be explicitly turned on if you require it.

MulticastSocket method (Java 2 v1.4 and higher):

public void setReuseAddress(boolean on) throws SocketException

---

The setReuseAddress() call takes a boolean argument, which is true if address reuse is to be enabled and false if address reuse is to be disabled. The method throws a SocketException if an error occurs enabling or disabling this socket option, or if the socket is closed. Assuming you have already created a MulticastSocket instance, this option is set like this:

```
try {
  sock.setReuseAddress(true);
} catch (SocketException se) {
  // add exception handling here
}
```

3.3.3   Adding Multicast Membership

Before a MulticastSocket can begin receiving multicast packets, it needs to send a join request to the multicast group. This join request results in two actions. First, the operating system will know to begin processing multicast packets for the group and passing them to the application. Second, an Internet Group Management Protocol (IGMP) join message is sent to the network, allowing any multicast forwarding tree additions needed to ensure packets for that group reach the host. For more details, see Section 2.3.4.

MulticastSocket methods:

```
public void joinGroup(InetAddress mcastaddr) throws IOException
public void joinGroup(SocketAddress mcastaddr, NetworkInterface netIf)
                      throws IOException
```

In Java, the joinGroup() method of the MulticastSocket class is used to send a join message. The method takes a single argument, which is the InetAddress of the multicast group to join. The joinGroup() call throws an IOException if there is an error joining the group or if the IP address passed to it is not a multicast address.

Here is sample code to join a multicast group on an existing MulticastSocket instance.

```
InetAddress mcAddress = InetAddress.getByName("239.255.10.10");

try {
  sock.joinGroup(mcAddress);
} catch (IOException ioe) {
  // add exception handling here
}
```

Multiple joins on different addresses are allowed, and Java does not specify any upper limit on the number of joins allowed on a single MulticastSocket.

In Java 2 v1.4 and higher, a joinGroup() call can take as an argument the new abstract class SocketAddress instead of an InetAddress, and it can take an additional argument of NetworkInterface to specify what local interface to join a group on.

3.3.4   Receiving Multicast Packets

Once a MulticastSocket has been created, the reuse address option has been set, and a multicast group has been joined, multicast packets can be received. In Java, this is done with the receive() method of the MulticastSocket class.

MulticastSocket method:

```
public void receive(DatagramPacket p) throws IOException
```

The receive() method takes a single argument, an instance of the DatagramPacket class where the incoming packet is to be stored. The datagram packet needs to be instantiated with a byte buffer before it is passed as an argument to receive(). The byte buffer must be large enough to accommodate the largest packet size or an exception will result. The code to do this is straightforward.

```
byte[] buf = new byte[1024];

DatagramPacket packet = new DatagramPacket(buf, buf.length);

try {
  sock.receive(packet);
} catch (IOException ioe) {
  // add exception handling here
}
```

The receive() call throws an IOException on error.

The DatagramPacket class has a set of methods used to retrieve both the data stored in it and metadata about the packet.

DatagramPacket selected methods:

```
public InetAddress getAddress();
public int getPort();
public byte[] getData();
public int getLength();
```

The getData() method is used to retrieve the byte buffer from the packet, and the getLength() method is used to get the length of that data. The getAddress() method is used to retrieve the IP address of the sending host. Here is an example of printing out the data and metadata associated with a DatagramPacket instance.

```
System.out.println("Received " + packet.getLength() +
    " bytes from " + packet.getAddress() + ": " +
    new String(packet.getData(), 0, packet.getLength()));
```

3.3.5   Dropping a Multicast Membership

Once a host is done receiving packets from a particular multicast group, it should send a drop membership request. This will both stop the operating system from passing packets destined for this group to the application and send an IGMP drop membership request. If the host is the last host on the subnet receiving this group's packets, the branches on the tree responsible for forwarding packets to the subnet will be pruned by the multicast routing protocol.

In Java, the drop membership request is sent using the leaveGroup() method of the MulticastSocket class.

MulticastSocket methods:

```
public void leaveGroup(InetAddress mcastaddr) throws IOException
public void leaveGroup(SocketAddress mcastaddr, NetworkInterface netIf)
                            throws IOException
```

The leaveGroup() method takes an InetAddress of the multicast group to be dropped. This method throws an IOException if there is an error leaving the group or the IP address argument is not a multicast address.

In Java 2 v1.4 and higher, a leaveGroup() can take as an argument the new abstract class SocketAddress instead of an InetAddress and can take an additional argument of NetworkInterface to specify what local interface to join a group on.

3.3.6 Multicast Receiver Code (Java Version)

Now that we have reviewed the Java multicast receiver classes and methods, we can present a complete example. Here is a quick recap of the steps involved in receiving multicast packets in Java.

1. Construct an instance of MulticastSocket.

2. Set the reuse address option using the MulticastSocket method setReuseOption() (optional).

3. Join the multicast group using the MulticastSocket method joinGroup().

4. Receive packets using the MulticastSocket method receive().

5. Drop the multicast group using the MulticastSocket method leaveGroup().

6. Close the socket using the close() method.

mcreceive.java

```
 1  import java.net.*;   /* import networking package */
 2  import java.io.*;    /* import input/output package */
 3
 4  public class mcreceive {
 5
 6    public static final int MAX_LEN  = 1024;  /* max receive buffer */
 7    public static final int MIN_PORT = 1024;  /* min network port */
 8    public static final int MAX_PORT = 65535; /* max network port */
 9
10    public static void main(String argv[]) {
11
12      InetAddress mcAddress=null; /* multicast address */
13      int mcPort=0;               /* multicast port */
14      int ttl=1;                  /* time to live */
```

```
15      boolean done=false;            /* variable for send loop */
16
17       /* validate number of arguments */
18      if (argv.length != 2) {
19        System.out.println("Usage: mcreceive " +
20                           "<Multicast IP> <Multicast Port>");
21        System.exit(1);
22      }
23
24      /* validate the multicast address argument */
25      try {
26        mcAddress = InetAddress.getByName(argv[0]);
27      } catch (UnknownHostException e) {
28        System.err.println(argv[0] + " is not a valid IP address");
29        System.exit(1);
30      }
31
32      /* validate address argument is a multicast IP */
33      if (! mcAddress.isMulticastAddress()) {
34        System.err.println(mcAddress.getHostAddress() +
35                           " is not a multicast IP address.");
36        System.exit(1);
37      }
38
39      /* parse and validate port argument */
40      try {
41        mcPort = Integer.parseInt(argv[1]);
42      } catch (NumberFormatException nfe) {
43        System.out.println("Invalid port number " + argv[1]);
44        System.exit(1);
45      }
46
47      if ((mcPort < MIN_PORT) || (mcPort > MAX_PORT)) {
48        System.out.println("Invalid port number " + mcPort);
49        System.out.println("Port should be in range " + MIN_PORT
50                           + " to " + MAX_PORT);
51        System.exit(1);
52      }
53
54      try {
55
56        /* instantiate a MulticastSocket */
57        MulticastSocket sock = new MulticastSocket(mcPort);
58
59        /* set the address reuse option */
60        sock.setReuseAddress(true); // Java 1.4 and higher
61
```

```
62          /* join the multicast group */
63          sock.joinGroup(mcAddress);
64
65       while (!done) {  /* loop forever */
66
67          /* create a new DatagramPacket with an empty buffer */
68          byte[] buf = new byte[MAX_LEN];
69          DatagramPacket packet = new DatagramPacket(buf, buf.length);
70
71          /* wait to receive packet into the DatagramPacket instance */
72          sock.receive(packet);
73
74          /* output the data from the packet received */
75          System.out.println("Received " + packet.getLength() +
76              " bytes from " + packet.getAddress() + ": "
77              + new String(packet.getData(),0,packet.getLength()));
78       }
79
80       sock.leaveGroup(mcAddress);
81       sock.close();
82
83     } catch (IOException e) {
84       System.err.println(e.toString());
85       System.exit(1);
86     }
87   }
88 }
```

mcreceive.java

Lines 1–2: Import the java.net and java.io packages for the networking and IO classes.

Lines 6–22: Standard variable declaration and argument validation.

Lines 24–30: Use the InetAddress method getByName() to create an InetAddress instance of the requested IP address. If the input is not a valid IP address, catch the UnknownHostException.

Lines 32–37: Use the InetAddress method isMulticastAddress() to ensure the IP argument is in the correct range for multicast.

Lines 39–52: Parse the port argument and throw an error if it is invalid. Verify that the port is in the valid range for user applications (1024 to 65535).

Lines 56–57: Create a new MulticastSocket. Catch the IOException in case of error.

Lines 59–60: Use the MulticastSocket method setReuseAddress() to allow multiple sockets on the same address and port.

Lines 62–63: Use the MulticastSocket method joinGroup() to join the multicast group.

Lines 67–69: Allocate an empty buffer and instantiate a DatagramPacket class with the buffer.

Lines 71–72: Use the MulticastSocket method receive() to block and receive a multicast packet.

Lines 74–77: Output the contents of the received packet.

Lines 80–81: Use the MulticastSocket methods leaveGroup() and close() to leave the multicast group and close the MulticastSocket. Since the membership will be dropped and the socket closed implicitly on program exit, these calls are not required, but it is always good practice to include them.

Lines 83–86: Catch any errors that may occur while populating and sending packets. Note that in this example we used one catch block for several method calls. If there is a need to catch individual errors and to perform different actions, this single catch block could be separated into multiple try/catch blocks.

3.4 A Sample Run

The mcsend application takes the multicast address and port to send to as arguments. Then everything typed on the command line is transmitted on that multicast address until Control-C is used to terminate the program.

```
% java mcsend 239.255.50.50 9000
Begin typing (return to send, Control-C to quit):
Testing123
Testing321
^C
```

The mcreceive application takes the multicast address and a port on which to listen as arguments. The program then continuously receives and prints to the terminal any packets received on that multicast address until terminated by Control-C.

```
% java mcreceive 239.255.50.50 9000
Received 10 bytes from 192.111.52.12: Testing123
Received 10 bytes from 192.111.52.12: Testing321
^C
```

3.5 Exercises

1. Using different hosts, try mixing and matching the Java and C multicast senders and receivers.

2. Assuming you are using Java 2 v1.4 or higher, try removing the setReuseAddress() call from the receiver code and running multiple copies of the program on the same host and same address/port. What errors do you receive?

3. Try adding additional joinGroup() calls in the receiver code and verify that you can receive from multiple groups on the same socket at once.

chapter **4**

Multicasting with .NET

This chapter introduces the basic classes and methods for multicast programming on Microsoft's .NET platform. .NET was introduced in 2001 and is a complete repackaging of all Microsoft's development architecture around an XML Web services platform. .NET includes some rearchitecting of existing Microsoft technologies and programming languages, and some new languages such as C#. The new .NET framework creates a largely unified class library for many Microsoft languages, including C#, C++, Visual Basic, and JScript (Microsoft's version of Javascript). This allows code from all these languages to be compiled into Microsoft Intermediate Language (MSIL) code, which is executed by a Common Language Runtime (CLR) execution environment. The .NET class library includes multicast-capable Socket and UdpClient classes that can be used across all these languages. The examples in this chapter are in Microsoft's new C# language, but the classes, methods, and properties will work in a similar way across all the .NET programming languages.[1]

As with our earlier chapters, we will introduce the C# multicast class library through a discussion of building simple multicast sender and receiver programs and then display annotated code for the entire programs.

4.1 The .NET Sockets Class

Like Java, C# provides classes and methods at a higher level and abstraction than C sockets. C# provides a class called UdpClient that contains UDP-specific socket functionality, including the ability to send multicast packets. However, the UdpClient class does not have all the multicast functionality a network programmer would expect. With UdpClient, socket options cannot be retrieved or set. For example, there is no capability to reuse an address, perform loopback, or specify Source Specific Multicast (SSM) sources (SSM will be discussed in Chapter 5). If these

---

[1] At the time of the writing of this book, the .NET class library was in beta 2. Check Microsoft's documentation at *msdn.microsoft.com* for updates and changes.

functions are not required, the UdpClient class should work just fine, and it is discussed briefly at the end of this chapter.

Luckily, the .NET API includes a more basic Sockets class that includes all the full-featured functionality necessary for multicast. This Sockets class is an object-oriented version of C sockets, matching most of the C API almost identically. One feature of the .NET API is that it can be used with minor modifications in almost all Microsoft programming languages, including C++, Visual Basic, and JScript.

Unless specifically stated otherwise, all the classes described in this chapter are part of the .NET namespace Systems.Net.Sockets. When programming an application, the use of the System.Net.Sockets namespace needs to be explicitly referenced at the beginning of the code.

```
using System.Net.Sockets;
```

4.2   Sending Multicast Packets in C#

We start by examining the four steps required to create a C# application that sends multicast packets.

1. Create a socket.

2. Optionally set the scope for the packets.

3. Send the data on the socket.

4. Close the socket.

Each step is detailed in the following sections.

4.2.1   Socket Creation and Destruction

The first step in sending multicast packets is to create a UDP socket using the C# Socket() class constructor.

System.Net.Sockets.Socket class

Class Constructor:

```
public Socket(AddressFamily addressFamily, SocketType socketType,
              ProtocolType protocolType);
```

Constructor Exception:

SocketException   Invalid combination of arguments or network error

Selected Method:

```
public void Close();
```

Table 4.1 C# Socket() call arguments.

Argument	Value	Meaning
AddressFamily	AddressFamily.InterNetwork	Internet address family
SocketType	SocketType.Dgram	Datagram socket
ProtocolType	ProtocolType.Udp	User datagram protocol

The socket is a handle to the local network endpoint, through which data can be received. The AddressFamily, SocketType, and ProtocolType classes all provide a list of member name constants to specify the type of socket to be opened (see Table 4.1). For a multicast socket, these will always be set to the same values.

These classes are enumerators, so the constants can be accessed without creating an instance of the associated class. A sample call to create a UDP datagram packet is as simple as

```
try {
  Socket s = new Socket(AddressFamily.InterNetwork,
                        SocketType.Dgram,
                        ProtocolType.Udp);
} catch (SocketException se) {
  Console.Error.WriteLine("Socket Exception: " + se.ToString());
  return 1;
}
```

As with Java, C# error handling is done by throwing exceptions. By including the call to the Socket constructor within a try block, any errors can be handled in the catch block.

4.2.2 Setting the Time-To-Live

The Time-To-Live (TTL) determines the number of multicast-enabled router hops a packet will be able to traverse before it is discarded. For a more detailed description of how TTLs work, see Section 2.2.3. In C#, as in C, the TTL is set and retrieved as a socket option. In C# that means the SetSocketOption() and GetSocketOption() methods.

Socket method SetSocketOption()

Method Overload List:

```
public void SetSocketOption(SocketOptionLevel optionLevel,
                            SocketOptionName optionName,
                            byte[] optionValue);

public void SetSocketOption(SocketOptionLevel optionLevel,
                            SocketOptionName optionName,
                            int optionValue);
```

```
public void SetSocketOption(SocketOptionLevel optionLevel,
                            SocketOptionName optionName,
                            object optionValue);
```

Method Exceptions:

SocketException   Network or operating system error
ObjectDisposedException   The Socket has been closed

SocketOptionLevel and SocketOptionName are enumerator classes that contain constant value names and do not need to be instantiated. To set the TTL, the socket option level is SocketOptionLevel.Socket, and the socket option name is SocketOptionName.MulticastTimeToLive. The SetSocketOption() method is overloaded to provide different argument types for the optionValue. To set the TTL, optionValue is used with an integer value. The default TTL if not otherwise set is 1, which will restrict the packets to the local LAN.

Assuming a Socket class object called sock has already been instantiated, the TTL can be set with the following code:

```
int ttl=5;

try {
  sock.SetSocketOption(SocketOptionLevel.Socket,
                       SocketOptionName.MulticastTimeToLive,
                       ttl);
} catch (SocketException se) {
  // error handling goes here
} catch (ObjectDisposedException ode) {
  // error handling goes here
}
```

SetSocketOption() can also be used to add and drop multicast group membership and to turn address reuse on. These functions will be discussed in Sections 4.3.4 and 4.3.6.

The value of a socket option can be retrieved using the Socket method GetSocketOption().

Socket method GetSocketOption()

Method Overload List:

```
public object GetSocketOption(SocketOptionLevel optionLevel,
                              SocketOptionName optionName);
public void GetSocketOption(SocketOptionLevel optionLevel,
                            SocketOptionName optionName,
                            byte[] optionValue);
public byte[] GetSocketOption(SocketOptionLevel optionLevel,
                              SocketOptionName optionName,
                              int optionLength);
```

Method Exceptions:

SocketException	Network or operating system error
ObjectDisposedException	The Socket has been closed

The GetSocketOption() method is overloaded to provide methods to get options of different value types. For the purposes of retrieving the integer TTL, the first prototype is used. An optionLevel argument and an optionName argument are provided as input, and an object type is returned. An object class in C# is malleable in the sense that it can be cast to different types. Since the TTL is an integer type, we cast the object to type int. In fact, the GetSocketOption() method almost always returns an integer except for a few specialized cases, which will be discussed later.

So, assuming that a Socket has already been created, the code to retrieve the TTL can be written as follows:

```
int ttl = (int) sock.GetSocketOption(SocketOptionLevel.IP,
              SocketOptionName.MulticastTimeToLive);

Console.WriteLine("SocketOptionName.MulticastTimeToLive = " + ttl);
```

4.2.3 Specifying Addresses in C#

At this point, we have not yet specified where we are sending packets. The next step is to specify the multicast address and port. Specifying the send address in C# involves creating an instance of the IPEndPoint class. There are two ways this class can take the IP address argument: as a long integer or as an instance of another class, IPAddress. Since user-provided IP addresses are typically not represented as long integers, the most intuitive way to instantiate an address is with the IPAddress class.

System.Net.IPAddress class

Class Constructor:

public IPAddress(long newAddress);

Selected Method:

public static IPAddress Parse(string ipString);

The IPAddress class also takes a long integer as its argument, but it has a Parse() method that will convert from an IP address string (in dotted quad notation) to an instance of IPAddress. Since the Parse() method is static, it can be called without instantiating an

IPAddress class. This allows an IPAddress class instance to be created in a single line of code like this:

```
IPAddress mcIP = IPAddress.Parse("239.255.10.10");
```

Once an IPAddress class exists, it can be used to create an IPEndPoint class instance.

System.Net.IPEndPoint class

Class Constructors:

```
public IPEndPoint(IPAddress address, int port);
public IPEndPoint(long address, int port);
```

Constructor Exceptions:

ArgumentOutOfRangeException	port < IPAddress.MinPort or port > IPAddress.MaxPort
ArgumentNullException	address is a null reference

Selected Public Field:

```
public static readonly IPAddress Any;
```

The IPAddress.Any field provides an IP address indicating that the server should listen for client activity on all network interfaces and is equivalent to 0.0.0.0.

An IPEndPoint instance can be created using the IPAddress instance and an integer port number as arguments, like this:

```
IPEndPoint ipep;
int        mcPort=20000;

IPAddress mcIP = IPAddress.Parse("239.255.10.10");

try {
  ipep = new IPEndPoint(mcIP, mcPort);
} catch (ArgumentNullException ex1) {
  // error handling here
} catch (ArgumentOutOfRangeException ex2) {
  // error handling here
}
```

4.2.4 Populating a C# Datagram Packet

The format of a datagram packet in C# is a simple array of bytes. For the purposes of our simple example, we are sending plain ASCII text as the payload of our packet. C# provides the ASCIIEncoding class that can provide the conversion from text to byte array.

System.Text.ASCIIEncoding class

Class Constructor:

public ASCIIEncoding();

Selected Methods:

public virtual byte[] GetBytes(string s);

The GetBytes() method is overloaded, but for our purposes we are interested in converting a string to a byte array. The ASCIIEncoding instance needs to be created; then the GetBytes() method can be called with a string argument, and it will return the byte array equivalent.

```
String str = "String to be converted";

ASCIIEncoding encode = new ASCIIEncoding();

byte[] convertedByteArray = encode.GetBytes(str);
```

4.2.5 Sending Multicast Packets

Now that a socket has been created, the TTL set, the address specified, and the packet populated, the packet is ready to be sent. The Socket class uses a SendTo() method for sending UDP packets.

Socket method SendTo()

Method Overload List:

```
public int SendTo(byte[] buffer, EndPoint remoteEP);
public int SendTo(byte[] buffer, SocketFlags socketFlags, EndPoint remoteEP);
public int SendTo(byte[] buffer, int size, SocketFlags socketFlags,
                  EndPoint remoteEP);
public int SendTo(byte[] buffer, int offset, int size,
                  SocketFlags socketFlags, EndPoint remoteEP);
```

Method Exceptions:

ArgumentNullException	The buffer parameter is null or the remoteEP parameter is a null reference
ArgumentOutOfRangeException	The specified offset or size exceeds the size of the buffer
SocketException	Operating system error
ObjectDisposedException	The Socket is closed

The SendTo() method takes a minimum of two arguments: a byte array buffer of data to send and an IPEndPoint address/port combination for the destination. Optional arguments include SocketFlags,[2] a data size, and a buffer offset at which to begin.

4.2.6 Multicast Sender Code (C# Version)

We are now ready to look at a complete C# multicast sender example. Just like the C and Java versions from the previous chapters, the MCSend.cs program takes standard input from the keyboard and sends it line by line to the multicast address specified. Control-C quits the program. The following is a quick recap of the steps involved:

1. Create a socket using Socket class.

2. Set the TTL using the Socket method SetSocketOption() (optional).

3. Send data using the Socket method SendTo().

4. Close the Socket using the Close() method.

MCSend.cs

```
1  using System;           // For Console and Exception classes
2  using System.Net;       // For IPAddress class
3  using System.Net.Sockets; // For Socket class
4
5  class MCSend {
6
7    const int MIN_PORT = 1024;  // min port value
8    const int MAX_PORT = 65535; // max port value
9
10   public static int Main(string[] args) {
11
12     Socket     sock;       // Multicast socket
13     IPAddress  mcIP;       // Destination multicast addr
14     int        mcPort;     // Destination port
15     IPEndPoint ipep;       // IP endpoint
16     int        ttl=1;      // time to live (1 hop)
17     Boolean    done=false; // loop variable
18
19     // Verify correct usage
20     if (args.Length != 2) {
21       Console.Error.WriteLine("Usage: MCSend " +
22                               "<Multicast IP> <Multicast Port>");
```

---

[2] Socket flags provide a variety of advanced options such as sending out-of-band (priority) data or peeking at the next packet without removing it from the queue. None of these flags are specific to multicast, and they are beyond the scope of this book to discuss.

```
23         return 1;
24      }
25
26      // Validate the input multicast IP address
27      try {
28         mcIP = IPAddress.Parse(args[0]);
29      } catch (Exception) {
30         Console.Error.WriteLine("Invalid IP Address specified.");
31         return 1;
32      }
33
34      // Validate the input port number
35      try {
36         mcPort = Int32.Parse(args[1]);
37      } catch(Exception) {
38         Console.Error.WriteLine("Invalid port specified.");
39         return 1;
40      }
41      if ((mcPort < MIN_PORT) || (mcPort > MAX_PORT)) {
42         Console.Error.WriteLine("Invalid port specified.");
43         Console.Error.WriteLine("Port must be between " + MIN_PORT
44                                 + " and " + MAX_PORT);
45         return 1;
46      }
47
48      // Create an IP endpoint class instance
49      ipep = new IPEndPoint(mcIP, mcPort);
50
51      try {
52
53         // Create the Socket
54         sock = new Socket(AddressFamily.InterNetwork,
55                           SocketType.Dgram,
56                           ProtocolType.Udp);
57
58         // Set the Time to Live
59         sock.SetSocketOption(SocketOptionLevel.IP,
60                              SocketOptionName.MulticastTimeToLive,
61                              ttl);
62
63         Console.WriteLine("Begin typing " +
64                           "(return to send, ctrl-C to quit):");
65
66         while (!done) {
67
68            // Read and format input from the terminal
69            string str = Console.ReadLine();
```

```
70
71              System.Text.ASCIIEncoding encode =
72                          new System.Text.ASCIIEncoding();
73
74          byte[] inputToBeSent = encode.GetBytes(str);
75
76          // Send the data packet
77          sock.SendTo(inputToBeSent, 0, inputToBeSent.Length,
78                      SocketFlags.None, ipep);
79      }
80
81      // Close the socket
82      sock.Close();
83
84    } catch (SocketException se) {
85      Console.Error.WriteLine("Socket Exception: "
86                          + se.ToString());
87      return 1;
88    } catch (Exception e) {
89      Console.Error.WriteLine("Exception: "
90                          + e.ToString());
91      return 1;
92    }
93    return 0;
94  }
95 }
```

MCSend.cs

Lines 1–3: Include the .NET libraries to be used.

Lines 7–24: Standard argument parsing and validation.

Lines 26–32: Use the IPAddress method Parse() to validate the IP address argument.

Lines 34–46: Use the Int32 method Parse() to validate the port is a valid integer. Verify that the port is in the valid range for user applications (1024 to 65535).

Lines 48–49: Create an IPEndPoint class instance with the destination multicast address and port.

Lines 53–56: Create the socket using the Socket() call. The constants used will always be the same: the address family is AddressFamily.InterNetwork, the socket type is Socket-Type.Dgram, and the protocol type is ProtocolType.UDP.

Lines 58–61: Set the Time-To-Live (hop count) using the SetSocketOption() method. In this program, we are setting the TTL to 1 to restrict traffic to the local subnet. Although 1 is the default TTL and does not need to be explicitly set, it is good practice to be explicit about the TTL.

Lines 68–74: Read the terminal input and convert it to a byte array in preparation for sending.

Lines 76–78: Send the data packet using the SendTo() method.

Lines 81–82: Close the socket when completed using the Close() call.
Lines 84–92: Basic error handling code.

4.2.7   Other Multicast Sender Options: Interface and Loopback

The two remaining options for multicast senders are setting the outgoing interface and whether to loop back transmitted packets.

For multihomed hosts, it may be useful to specify the outgoing interface when sending packets. This is done with the Socket method SetSocketOption() using the MulticastInterface option name. The interface is set and retrieved as an integer representing the interface. The code to set the interface looks like the following:

```
int interface = (int)sock.GetSocketOption(SocketOptionLevel.IP,
                                SocketOptionName.MulticastInterface);

Console.WriteLine("Default interface = " + interface);

interface++;

sock.SetSocketOption(SocketOptionLevel.IP,
                    SocketOptionName.MulticastInterface,
                    interface);
```

Multicast loopback determines whether a sender to a group can also receive its own packets sent to the group. This value is toggled using the Socket method SetSocketOption() with the MulticastLoopback option name. The loopback is set and retrieved as an integer representing enabled (1) or disabled (0). The default value is enabled (1). The code to check the current value of loopback and then disable it is as follows:

```
int loopback = (int)sock.GetSocketOption(SocketOptionLevel.IP,
                                SocketOptionName.MulticastLoopback);

Console.WriteLine("Current loopback = " + loopback);

loopback = 0;

sock.SetSocketOption(SocketOptionLevel.IP,
                    SocketOptionName.MulticastLoopback,
                    loopback);
```

4.3   Receiving Multicast Packets in C#

Now that we have described the code to send multicast packets in C#, we will examine the steps involved in receiving multicast packets.

1. Create a socket.

2. Optionally set the port reuse socket option.

3. Bind to the socket.

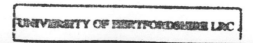

4. Join the multicast group.

5. Receive multicast data.

6. Drop the multicast group.

7. Close the socket.

Each step is detailed in the following sections.

4.3.1   Socket Creation and Destruction

The first step is to create an instance of the Socket class, specifying a UDP datagram socket.

```
try {
  Socket s = new Socket(AddressFamily.InterNetwork,
                        SocketType.Dgram,
                        ProtocolType.Udp);
} catch (SocketException se) {
  Console.Error.WriteLine("Socket Exception: " + se.ToString());
  return 1;
}
```

This code is identical to the Socket creation for the multicast sender (or any UDP socket for that matter), so we will not repeat the class definition here.

4.3.2   Setting the Address Reuse Option

By default more than one process on the same host cannot bind to the same address. In unicast, this makes perfect sense, but in the one-to-many world of multicast, there may be a need to have multiple applications receive packets arriving on a particular port. If this function is necessary, the address reuse socket option should be set to "on." This is done using the Socket class method SetSocketOption(), the same method used to set the TTL. For this option, the option level is SocketOptionLevel.Socket, the option name is SocketOptionName.ReuseAddress, and the option value is the integer value 1 (indicating "true" or "on"). Assuming a Socket instance has already been created, the code to turn address reuse on is

```
sock.SetSocketOption(SocketOptionLevel.Socket,
                     SocketOptionName.ReuseAddress,
                     1);
```

The current value of the reuse address option can be retrieved using the Socket method GetSocketOption(). Again, assuming a Socket instance has already been created, the value can be retrieved using the following code:

```
int value = (int) sock.GetSocketOption(SocketOptionLevel.Socket,
                                       SocketOptionName.ReuseAddress);

if (value == 1) {
  Console.WriteLine("ReuseAddress option is set.");
```

```
} else {
  Console.WriteLine("ReuseAddress option is not set.");
}
```

Note that GetSocketOption() with these arguments returns an object and must be explicitly cast to an int for the ReuseAddress option.

4.3.3 Binding an Address to a Socket

In order for an application to inform the system that datagrams for a particular port should be forwarded to the application, it must execute a bind on the port. The Socket method Bind() provides this functionality.

Socket method Bind()

Method Prototype:

```
public void Bind(EndPoint localEP);
```

Method Exceptions:

ArgumentNullException	The localEP parameter is a null reference
SocketException	Operating system error
ObjectDisposedException	The Socket is closed

The Bind() call is used to specify a local network endpoint, but the real result of issuing this call is to inform the operating system that an application would like to receive datagrams on the requested port number. With C, some operating systems do not require the bind. However, in C# the bind is always required. Failure to include the bind will cause the ReceiveFrom() call (defined later) to fail with the following somewhat misleading SocketException:

```
An invalid argument was supplied at System.Net.Sockets.Socket.ReceiveFrom
```

The argument to the Bind() call is an instance of the IPEndPoint class, defined earlier in the multicast sender section. An IPEndPoint instance contains both IP address and port data, and while we want to specify the receive port, the receive IP address with multicast can be any IP. In order to bind to a wildcard IP address, we use a property of the IPAddress class called Any. If a Socket instance has already been created, the code to bind a socket to a local endpoint is

```
// my multicast receive port is 20000
int mcPort=20000;

// create an IPEndPoint on any incoming interface and port 20000
IPEndPoint ipep = new IPEndPoint(IPAddress.Any, mcPort);

// Bind the socket
try {
```

```
    sock.Bind(ipep);
} catch (SocketException ex1) {
    // error handling goes here
} catch (ObjectNullException ex2) {
    // error handling goes here
} catch (ObjectDisposedException ex3) {
    // error handling goes here
}
```

When Bind() is called, the LocalEndPoint property of the socket is set to the value of the IPEndPoint argument of the Bind() call.

4.3.4   Adding Multicast Membership

In order to receive packets for a given multicast group, membership must be added (or "subscribed to") for the group. With C# sockets, this is done by sending an AddMembership request using the Socket method SetSocketOption().

When requesting an AddMembership, the option level is SocketOptionLevel.IP and the option name is SocketOptionName.AddMembership. The SocketValue is an instance of a new class called, appropriately enough, MulticastOption.

System.Net.Sockets.MulticastOption class

Class Constructors:

```
public MulticastOption(IPAddress group);
public MulticastOption(IPAddress group, IPAddress mcint);
```

Constructor Exception:

ArgumentNullException   Either group or mcint is a null reference

---

A MulticastOption instance consists of an IPAddress of the multicast group to be added and an optional IPAddress of an interface that the add should be applied to (used for multi-homed hosts). If the Socket instance (sock) has already been created, the code to join a multicast group would be

```
IPAddress mcIP = IPAddress.Parse("239.255.10.10");

sock.SetSocketOption(SocketOptionLevel.IP,
                SocketOptionName.AddMembership,
                new MulticastOption(mcIP));
```

GetSocketOption() does not support getting existing multicast memberships.

4.3.5   Receiving Multicast Packets

Receiving multicast packets is achieved using the ReceiveFrom() method of the Socket class.

Socket method ReceiveFrom()

Method Overload List:

```
public int ReceiveFrom(byte[] buffer, ref EndPoint remoteEP);
public int ReceiveFrom(byte[] buffer, SocketFlags socketFlags,
                    ref EndPoint remoteEP);
public int ReceiveFrom(byte[] buffer, int size, SocketFlags socketFlags,
                    ref EndPoint remoteEP);
public int ReceiveFrom(byte[] buffer, int offset, int size,
                    SocketFlags socketFlags, ref EndPoint remoteEP);
```

Method Exceptions:

ArgumentNullException	The buffer parameter is a null reference or the remoteEP parameter is a null reference
ArgumentOutOfRangeException	The size parameter exceeds the size of the buffer
SocketException	Operating system error
ObjectDisposedException	The Socket is closed

The ReceiveFrom() method is overloaded to provide different functionality. At a minimum, the method takes a buffer array where the incoming packet can be stored and a reference to the remote sending EndPoint (more on this in a moment). Optional arguments include an offset within the buffer to begin storing the data, a maximum size of data to receive, and socket flag options. ReceiveFrom() is normally a blocking call, meaning it will wait until a packet has been received before proceeding. ReceiveFrom returns an integer value equal to the number of bytes received.

When receiving packets in C#, the ReceiveFrom() method requires a reference to an EndPoint class as a parameter. When passing the EndPoint as an argument to ReceiveFrom(), it is initialized with the IPAddress.Any property since the remote host could be an IP address. After the ReceiveFrom() call, the EndPoint instance will hold the IP address and port of the host that sent the packet. The IP and port can be output using the EndPoint method ToString(). The EndPoint class is a more generic supertype of the IPEndPoint class we have already seen, and in fact we can take an IPEndPoint instance and cast it to an EndPoint in order to use it as an argument to ReceiveFrom().

```
// Create an IPEndPoint for IPAddress Any
IPEndPoint remoteIPEndPoint = new IPEndPoint(IPAddress.Any, 0);
```

```
// Cast the IPEndPoint to a generic EndPoint
EndPoint remoteEndPoint = (EndPoint)remoteIPEndPoint;

// Create a buffer to receive the packet
byte[] recData = newByte[1024];

try {
  // Block to receive a packet
  int len = sock.ReceiveFrom(recData, ref remoteEndPoint);

  // Output the ASCII contents of the packet received
  ASCIIEncoding encode = new ASCIIEncoding();
  Console.WriteLine("Data received from " + remoteEndPoint.ToString());
  Console.WriteLine(encode.GetString(recData, 0, len));

} catch (SocketException ex1) {
  // error handling goes here
} catch (ArgumentNullException ex2) {
  // error handling goes here
} catch (ObjectDisposedException ex3) {
  // error handling goes here
} catch (ArgumentOutOfRangeException ex4) {
  // error handling goes here
}
```

4.3.6   Dropping a Multicast Membership

Once a receiver is done listening on a particular multicast group, membership in the group should be dropped. This serves the dual purpose of stopping the operating system from passing packets destined to the group to the application, and also sending an IGMP message to the local subnet informing the router that membership in the group has been dropped. If the group member leaving the group was the last member on the subnet, the router will initiate action to prune the local branch of the tree and not forward traffic to the subnet anymore.

If the Socket instance has already been created and the membership added, this sample code shows how a membership can be dropped using SetSocketOption() with the Drop-Membership option:

```
IPAddress mcIP = IPAddress.Parse("239.255.10.10");

sock.SetSocketOption(SocketOptionLevel.IP,
                     SocketOptionName.DropMembership,
                     new MulticastOption(mcIP));
```

4.3.7   Multicast Receiver Code (C# Version)

We are now ready to look at the complete C# multicast receiver example. Just like the C and Java versions from the last two chapters, the MCReceive.cs program listens on a specified multicast address and port and outputs the data it receives to the console. Control-C quits the program. The steps involved are as follows:

1. Create a socket using the Socket class.

2. Set the address reuse option using the Socket method SetSocketOption() (optional).

3. Bind the socket using the Socket method Bind().

4. Join the multicast group using AddMembership with the Socket method SetSocketOption().

5. Receive data using the Socket method ReceiveFrom().

6. Drop the multicast group using DropMembership with the Socket method SetSocket-Option().

7. Close the Socket using the Close() method.

MCReceive.cs

```
1   using System;          // For Console and Exception classes
2   using System.Net;      // For IPAddress class
3   using System.Net.Sockets; // For Socket class
4
5   class MCReceive {
6
7     const int MIN_PORT = 1024;  // min port value
8     const int MAX_PORT = 65535; // max port value
9
10    public static int Main(string[] args) {
11
12      Socket      sock;         // Multicast socket
13      IPAddress   mcIP;         // Multicast group to join
14      int         mcPort;       // Port to receive on
15      IPEndPoint  receivePoint; // IP endpoint
16      int         MAX_LEN=1024; // Max receive buffer size
17      Boolean     done=false;   // loop variable
18
19      // Verify correct usage
20      if (args.Length != 2) {
21        Console.Error.WriteLine("Usage: MCReceive " +
22                        "<Multicast IP> <Multicast Port>");
23        return 1;
24      }
25
26      // Validate the input multicast IP address
27      try {
28        mcIP = IPAddress.Parse(args[0]);
29      } catch (Exception) {
30        Console.Error.WriteLine("Invalid IP Address specified.");
```

```
31          return 1;
32      }
33
34      // Validate the input port number
35      try {
36          mcPort = Int32.Parse(args[1]);
37      } catch(Exception) {
38          Console.Error.WriteLine("Invalid Port specified.");
39          return 1;
40      }
41      if ((mcPort < MIN_PORT) || (mcPort > MAX_PORT)) {
42          Console.Error.WriteLine("Invalid Port specified.");
43          Console.Error.WriteLine("Port must be between " + MIN_PORT
44                                  + " and " + MAX_PORT);
45          return 1;
46      }
47
48      try {
49
50          // Create the Socket
51          sock = new Socket(AddressFamily.InterNetwork,
52                            SocketType.Dgram,
53                            ProtocolType.Udp);
54
55          // Set the reuse address option
56          sock.SetSocketOption(SocketOptionLevel.Socket,
57                              SocketOptionName.ReuseAddress, 1);
58
59          // Create an IPEndPoint and bind to it
60          IPEndPoint ipep=new IPEndPoint(IPAddress.Any, mcPort);
61          sock.Bind(ipep);
62
63          // Add membership in the multicast group
64          sock.SetSocketOption(SocketOptionLevel.IP,
65                              SocketOptionName.AddMembership,
66                              new MulticastOption(mcIP, IPAddress.Any));
67
68          // Create the EndPoint class
69          receivePoint = new IPEndPoint(IPAddress.Any, 0);
70          EndPoint tempReceivePoint = (EndPoint)receivePoint;
71
72          while (!done) {
73              byte[] recData = new byte[MAX_LEN];
74
75              // Receive the multicast packets
76              int length = sock.ReceiveFrom(recData, 0, MAX_LEN,
77                                          SocketFlags.None,
```

```
78                                 ref tempReceivePoint);
79
80          // Format and output the received data packet
81          System.Text.ASCIIEncoding encode =
82                              new System.Text.ASCIIEncoding();
83          Console.WriteLine("Received " + length + " bytes from " +
84                          tempReceivePoint.ToString() + ": " +
85                          encode.GetString(recData, 0, length));
86        }
87
88        // Drop membership
89        sock.SetSocketOption(SocketOptionLevel.IP,
90                          SocketOptionName.DropMembership,
91                          new MulticastOption(mcIP,
92                                      IPAddress.Any));
93
94        // Close the socket
95        sock.Close();
96
97      } catch (SocketException se) {
98        Console.Error.WriteLine("Socket Exception: " + se.ToString());
99        return 1;
100     } catch (Exception e) {
101       Console.Error.WriteLine("Exception: " + e.ToString());
102       return 1;
103     }
104     return 0;
105   }
106 }
```

MCReceive.cs

Lines 1–3: Include the .NET libraries to be used.

Lines 7–24: Standard argument parsing and validation.

Lines 26–32: Use the IPAddress method Parse() to validate the IP address argument.

Lines 34–46: Use the Int32 method Parse() to validate the port is a valid integer. Verify that the port is in the valid range for user applications (1024 to 65535).

Lines 50–53: Create the socket using the Socket() call. The constants used will always be the same: AddressFamily is InterNetwork, SocketType is Dgram, and ProtocolType is UDP.

Lines 55–57: Set the reuse address option using the SetSocketOption() method. This will allow multiple receivers to be run on the same host without conflict.

Lines 59–61: Create an IPEndPoint instance with the port to receive on and the constant IPAddress.Any, indicating any incoming interface can be used. If there is a need to specify a particular interface, it would be done in this part of the code. However, in most cases an application will want to hear multicast packets that come in on any interface. Once this class is created, it is used to bind to the port with the Bind() method.

Lines 63–66: Add membership in the multicast group by using a SetSocketOption() call using the AddMembership option. The argument is an instance of the MulticastOption class, which takes the multicast IP address and an optional interface address in its constructor.

Lines 67–70: Create an EndPoint class instance, again using the port to listen to and the constant IPAddress.Any. After the ReceiveFrom() call, the EndPoint will hold the IP address and port of the host that sent the packet.

Lines 75–78: Receive the multicast packets using the ReceiveFrom() method.

Lines 80–86: Format and output the data packet contents.

Lines 88–92: When done receiving packets, a multicast receiver should drop membership in the group with a SetSocketOption() method call using the DropMembership option and close the socket with the Close() call. Since the program will exit after these calls, the explicit drop membership and close are not required, but it is good practice to include them.

Lines 97–103: Basic exception handling code.

4.4 A Sample Run: C# Multicast Sender and Receiver

The MCSend program takes the multicast address and port on which to send as arguments. Then everything typed on the command line is transmitted on that multicast address until Control-C is used to terminate the program.

```
C:\>MCSend.exe 239.255.50.50 10000
Begin typing (return to send, ctrl-C to quit):
Testing123
Testing321
^C
```

The MCReceive application takes the multicast address and port to listen on as arguments. The program then receives and echos on standard out any packets received on that multicast address until terminated by hitting Control-C.

```
C:\>MCReceive.exe 239.255.50.50 10000
Received 10 bytes from 239.255.50.50:10000: Testing123
Received 10 bytes from 239.255.50.50:10000: Testing321
^C
```

4.5 C# and Source Specific Multicast

So far, we have discussed the C# classes and methods for Any Source Multicast (ASM). C# also provides a few additional methods for Source Specific Multicast (SSM). From a programmatic point of view, SSM is an extension of the ASM methods we have already discussed. SSM methods are currently available only for C# on the Windows XP platform. The additional SSM methods are described in detail in Chapter 5.

4.6 The C# UdpClient **Class**

C# also provides a UdpClient class, which is a higher-level abstraction of a UDP socket. The UdpClient class is not as flexible as the Socket class and does not allow the direct setting of SetSocketOption() values. Some of the socket options that are crucial to multicast have been given their own methods under the UdpClient class, such as setting the TTL and joining and dropping multicast group membership. Other options such as setting the loopback, address reuse, or Source Specific Multicast functionality are not available, however.

Despite its limitations, there may be instances where the simpler UdpClient class can be used for a multicast program that does not require any of these advanced options. We briefly present the API for the UdpClient class here.

4.6.1 Socket Creation and Destruction

The UdpClient class creates a socket with a UdpClient constructor and closes a socket with a Close() method.

System.Net.Sockets.UdpClient class

Class Constructors:

```
public UdpClient();
public UdpClient(int port);
public UdpClient(IPEndPoint localEP);
public UdpClient(string hostname, int port);
```

Constructor Exceptions:

ArgumentException	The port parameter is > MaxPort or < MinPort
ArgumentNullException	Either localEP or hostname is a null reference
SocketException	An error occurred while connecting to the remote host

---

The UdpClient class is used to create a socket, a handle to the network endpoint for sending or receiving UDP data (including multicast). The constructor call takes an optional address and port as an argument. An alternative optional argument is a local interface IP address, which can be used to specify the outgoing interface for a multihomed host.

Once an application is done with a socket, it should be closed with a Close() method call so its resources can be reclaimed by the system.

UdpClient method Close()

Method Prototype:

public void Close()

Method Exception:

SocketException   An error occurred while closing the socket

The UdpClient constructor and its Close() method throw a SocketException on error.

4.6.2   Connecting and Binding with UdpClient

If the address and port number are included in the call to the UdpClient constructor, the bind is implicit. If the address and port are not included in the UdpClient constructor call, these values will need to be specified in a separate call to the Connect() method. The Connect() method will then perform the bind.

UdpClient method Connect()

Method Overload List:

```
public void Connect(IPAddress addr, int port);
public void Connect(string hostname, int port);
public void Connect(IPEndPoint endPoint);
```

Method Exceptions:

ArgumentException   The port parameter is > MaxPort or < MinPort
ArgumentNullException   Either localEP or hostname is a null reference
SocketException   An error occurred while connecting to the remote host

---

The Connect() method allows a target host and port to be set (or reset) for UDP packets. The target host can be either a string hostname or an IP address in the form of an IPAddress class instance. The outgoing interface for multihomed hosts can also be set by passing an IPEndPoint class instance.

4.6.3   Joining and Dropping Multicast Groups / Setting the TTL

The UdpClient API for joining and dropping multicast groups and setting the TTL is a bit confusing. As we have discussed, joining and dropping multicast groups apply to multicast receivers, and setting the TTL applies to multicast senders. Despite that, in the UdpClient class, Microsoft has opted to combine the two options into a single method. The JoinMulticastGroup() method of the UdpClient class takes an IPAddress of the group to join, and optionally a TTL. No other method of setting the TTL is available in the UdpClient class. While it is true that multicast senders are often also receivers, this is not always the case and certainly should not be required. When using the .NET UdpClient class, however, a multicast group will have to be joined in order to set the TTL for transmitted packets.

UdpClient method JoinMulticastGroup()

Method Overload List:

```
public void JoinMulticastGroup(IPAddress multicastAddr);
public void JoinMulticastGroup(IPAddress multicastAddr, int timeToLive);
```

Method Exceptions:

ArgumentOutOfRangeException	The TTL provided is not between 0 and 255
ObjectDisposedException	The underlying Socket has been closed
SocketException	The Socket was unable to join the multicast group

For multicast receivers, JoinMulticastGroup() will need to be called before packets will be received from a specified multicast address. For multicast senders, JoinMulticastGroup() will need to be called if the desired TTL value is anything other than the default value of 1.

UdpClient method DropMulticastGroup()

Method Prototype:

```
public void DropMulticastGroup(IPAddress multicastAddr);
```

Method Exceptions:

ObjectDisposedException	The underlying Socket has been closed
SocketException	The Socket was unable to join the multicast group

The DropMulticastGroup() method is called when an application is done receiving packets from a specified multicast address. This method takes a single argument, which is the IPAddress of the multicast address to be dropped.

4.6.4   Sending Multicast Packets

Once the UdpClient has been created and bound and the TTL is set, an application can begin
sending packets. Packets are sent using the Send() method of the UdpClient class.

UdpClient method Send()

Method Overload List:

```
public int Send(byte[] dgram, int bytes)
public int Send(byte[] dgram, int bytes, IPEndPoint endPoint)
public int Send(byte[] dgram, int bytes, string hostname, int port)
```

Method Exceptions:

ArgumentException	The dgram parameter is a null reference
InvalidOperationException	UdpClient is already connected to a remote host
ObjectDisposedException	The underlying Socket has been closed
SocketException	An error occurred while sending data to the Socket

The Send() method takes a byte array of data and optional fields for the number of bytes
to send, the interface to send on, or the hostname and port of the destination. Send() returns
an integer of the number of bytes that were sent.

4.6.5   Receiving Multicast Packets

Once a UdpClient instance has been created and bound, and once the multicast group has
been joined using JoinMulticastGroup(), the application is ready to receive packets. Packets
are received using the Receive() method.

UdpClient method Receive()

Method Prototype:

```
public byte[] Receive(ref IPEndPoint remoteEP);
```

Method Exceptions:

ObjectDisposedException	The underlying Socket has been closed
SocketException	An error occurred while reading the Socket

The Receive() method takes a single IPEndPoint argument. The IPEndPoint represents
the remote host from which data is to be received going into the call. In the case of multicast,

this endpoint will be set to either the multicast IP address or the constant IPAddress.Any and the port number. Upon receipt of a packet, the IPEndPoint contains the IP address of the host that sent the packet. The return value of Receive() is the packet received as a byte array.

4.6.6 Sender Sample Code

```
UdpClient sender;
IPAddress mcIP;
int mcPort=10000;
int ttl=5;
byte packet[5]="data";

mcIP = IPAddress.Parse("239.255.10.10");

try {
  sender = new UdpClient(mcIP, mcPort);

  /* set the TTL */
  sender.JoinMulticastGroup(mcIP, ttl);

  int bytesSent = sender.Send(packet, packet.Length);

  sender.DropMulticastGroup(mcIP);

  sender.Close();
} catch (SocketException se) {
  // error handling here
}
```

4.6.7 Receiver Sample Code

```
UdpClient receiver;
IPAddress mcIP;
int mcPort=10000;
IPEndPoint receivePoint;

mcIP = IPAddress.Parse("239.255.10.10");

try {
  receiver = new UdpClient(mcPort);

  receiver.JoinMulticastGroup(mcIP);

  receivePoint = new IPEndPoint(mcIP, mcPort);

  byte[] recData = receiver.Receive(ref receivePoint);

  receiver.DropMulticastGroup(mcIP);

  receiver.Close();
```

```
} catch (SocketException se) {
  // error handling here
}
```

4.7 Exercises

1. One of the overloaded arguments for the `Socket` method `ReceiveFrom()` is a size field. It would be logical to assume that setting the size argument to your maximum buffer size would prevent buffer overflows. Try lowering the `MAX_LEN` variable and sending a packet that exceeds the value. What are the results? How could you test for and handle this condition?

2. Try running multiple copies of senders and receivers in all the different languages (C, Java, and C#). How do they interact?

3. Try commenting out the `ReuseAddress` call in the receiver code and running multiple copies of the program on the same host. What kinds of errors do you get?

chapter 5

Source Specific Multicast

Until now, we have focused on a type of multicast called Any Source Multicast (ASM). In Chapters 2 through 4, all the examples were presented using the ASM version of multicast. We now turn our attention to a new version of multicast called Source Specific Multicast (SSM).

Luckily, most of the differences between ASM and SSM occur in how multicast trees are built. In other words, ASM versus SSM has almost no effect on how applications are programmed. However, there is one simple, but major, difference for applications.

The key difference between ASM and SSM has to do with whether it is the responsibility of the application to know the IP addresses of the source(s) or whether it is the responsibility of the network whose sources are transmitting. SSM puts a slightly heavier burden on the application programmer, but the trade-off of not having to do source discovery at the network layer is a significant advantage.

Therefore, as we will show in this chapter, the programming task becomes one of discovering the source(s) for a group and then passing this information via the socket interface.

5.1 Source Specific Multicast Defined

ASM is the original service model developed by Deering in the late 1980s [11, 12]. In the ASM approach, when a host joins a group, it will receive all sources transmitting packets to the group. One benefit of this kind of join is that an application joining a group does not need to even know who the sources are before it joins the group. The network is assumed to do all the work.

In late 2000, attempts were made to create a new service model. This new model was called Source Specific Multicast (SSM) [24]. SSM means that a multicast group is identified not only by the multicast IP address, but also by the unicast IP address of the source (or sources). As we will see in this chapter, this approach provides additional functionality (and protection) that was lacking in ASM. Of course, this comes at a cost. The application must now discover who the sources it wants to listen to are. Instead of sending a join message for just a group, a host must send a message joining a specific source and group. And, of course, if a host wants to join a group with multiple sources, multiple join messages are needed.

SSM is an open standard that is in the final stages of becoming an Internet Engineering Task Force (IETF) Request for Comments (RFC). SSM enjoys wide industry support, and it appears that SSM will become a very important part of multicast in the Internet. Unfortunately, SSM requires support in routers and in hosts through the application programming interface. Networking vendors are rapidly adding router support, but host support is not yet widespread. It may be some time before SSM support becomes ubiquitous. For this reason, we have separated the discussion of how SSM works and the programming API to use it into a separate chapter. For a more detailed discussion of how SSM works in the network and the key differences from ASM, see Appendix A.

5.1.1   The (Source, Group) Pair Notation

In talking about both ASM and SSM, it is helpful to use a common notation called a (source, group) pair (often pronounced "S-comma-G-pair"). When joining a group in ASM, there is no notion of source for the purposes of defining the group. Therefore, the group is referred to as (*,G) (pronounced "star-comma-G"), that is, all sources for group G. With SSM, the source is included in the group definition, creating an (S,G) group, often called a channel. An example of such a channel is (192.111.52.12, 232.1.3.5). This refers to a group where the multicast address is 232.1.3.5 and the source is host 192.111.52.12. When a receiver joins this channel in SSM, it can expect that it will receive packets sent only from source host 192.111.52.12. If any other host attempts to send to this channel, its packets will not be received by anyone on the channel (192.111.52.12, 232.1.3.5)—essentially because the new host forms a new channel to which our host never joined.

The way to distinguish between ASM and SSM is based on the multicast group address. ASM and SSM have nonoverlapping ranges of addresses. Basically, SSM is 232/8 (232.0.0.0 to 232.255.255.255) and ASM is everything else in 224/4. See Chapter 6 for more details on addressing.

Certainly, there are some interesting questions about what happens if an application tries to send an "ASM join" to an SSM channel and vice versa. Unfortunately, an in-depth discussion of this topic is beyond the scope of this book. However, this issue has been discussed in a recently published research paper [3].

5.2   Advantages of SSM

There are a number of advantages that SSM has over ASM. Some of the most important are the ability to filter unwanted sources, address collision avoidance, route optimization, and reduced inter-domain infrastructure to support multicast. We discuss each of these in more detail.

5.2.1 Filtering of Sources

One of the major advantages of SSM is the ability to join only specific sources of interest. This functionality has been unavailable in ASM until only very recently. In ASM, any source could send to a group address, and all connected receivers listening to that group would have to receive the packets. This could potentially be very bad. Consider, for example, someone trying to watch a videoconference when a malicious source joins the group and sends many megabits per second of garbage. The network and many of the group's receivers would likely be overwhelmed.

The ability to distinguish between sources is a level of granularity that is provided through the Internet Group Management Protocol (IGMP). Essentially, SSM requires IGMPv3, while ASM works with both IGMPv2 [20] and IGMPv3 [8]. It is IGMPv3 that allows the host to send source-specific information along with the group address [23].

The ability to filter sources should not be confused with security. While it eliminates some of the most obvious sources of attack, a few are still available. For example, a malicious source could still spoof the source IP of a valid sender and find a way to get malicious packets onto the multicast tree—either an ASM tree or an SSM tree. However, the ability to filter sources does provide a mechanism to prevent unintentional mixing of group traffic and a way to filter a source transmitting unwanted multicast traffic.

5.2.2 Address Collision Avoidance

As we will discuss in Chapter 6, there is no universally implemented and accepted mechanism for avoiding address collision in the multicast address space. Source Specific Multicast is an enormous enhancement in this area because the source IP defines the group in addition to the multicast group address. For example, with SSM, a group on (192.111.52.12, 232.1.3.5) is different from a group on (192.111.52.13, 232.1.3.5). While these groups would "collide" and receive each other's traffic using ASM, they will not with SSM. This greatly expands the universe of nonconflicting multicast address space and allows each source to be responsible for ensuring that groups are unique. Basically, each host has the full 2^{24} set of addresses (all of the 232/8 range) to use without conflicting with any other host.

5.2.3 Route Optimization and Reduced Infrastructure

In the main part of this book, we have tried to avoid too many details of how multicast routing works inside the network, but it is useful to see a brief explanation of how SSM makes multicast routing easier.

With ASM, multicast trees that span networks are centered on well-known routers, called rendezvous points (RPs). These RPs become the hub where a multicast tree is rooted and through which all multicast traffic is routed (initially at least). Sources send their multicast packets to these RPs, and receivers' IGMP requests trigger the sending of routing protocol join messages that are sent to these RPs. Initial multicast data also flows through RPs. Most multicast routing protocols have been optimized to then switch to a tree rooted at the source if that is how the network administrator wants the network to operate. All this infrastructure is necessary because when a receiver joins a group, it does not know who or where the sources are.

In SSM, the application already knows the source, or must discover this information. As a result, the network can forgo all the infrastructure and state. Sources do not have to advertise to the RP. Receivers do not have to subscribe to the RP. In fact, RPs do not need to exist at all. Instead, each receiver simply joins a channel. The multicast group and source address are used to build a reverse shortest path back to the source. Join messages from all a group's receivers work to form a reverse shortest path tree. This also means the intermediate step where the multicast tree goes through the RP is bypassed.

5.3   Host Support for SSM

In order for a host to support SSM, it must support version 3 of the Internet Group Management Protocol (IGMPv3) [8]. Currently, few operating systems support this out of the box. One notable exception is Microsoft Windows XP, which provides native IGMPv3 support along with programming extensions in the .NET framework. For most Unix-based systems, kernel patches to add IGMPv3 support are becoming available (Linux and FreeBSD are available now); check with your vendor or at any other popular (and reputable) site on the Internet. Another alternative is IGMPv3-lite, which is a stand-alone daemon program from Cisco systems that provides IGMPv3 support by intercepting IGMP messages. See Cisco's Web site for information on this service.

5.4   SSM Additions to the APIs

When it comes to the programmer's view of SSM implementation, the differences from ASM are surprisingly small. The only change to the API is the need to specify a source IP address in addition to a multicast group address. This is done using a new set of socket options. Unix systems with IGMPv3 support will typically have the proper C headers and libraries installed to support SSM in C code. The Microsoft .NET libraries contain SSM options, and we describe the C# version. At the time of this book's writing, Java has no extensions available to support SSM.

5.4.1   SSM in C

The recommended socket changes to support SSM are described in the Internet Draft "Socket Interface Extensions for Multicast Source Filters" [35]. This document describes two APIs: a basic API known as the delta-based API, and an advanced API known as the full-state API.

Basic (Delta-Based) API

The basic API is called delta based because it allows changes (deltas) in an incremental way (i.e., sources are added or removed one at a time). The basic API has two different modes:

- **Any source (inclusive):** All sources are accepted by default, but individual sources can be removed or added over time.

- **Controlled source (exclusive):** All sources are denied by default; individual sources can be added or removed over time.

The mode a particular socket is in depends on which socket option specific to the mode is set first. If the any-source socket option is set first, the socket is in any-source mode for the duration of its lifetime. Any attempt to set a controlled-source socket option on that socket will result in an error. Likewise, if the controlled-source option is set first, the socket will be in controlled-source mode for the duration of its lifetime. Any attempt to set an any-source option on that socket will result in an error.

For the any-source mode, two new socket options are introduced: IP_BLOCK_SOURCE and IP_UNBLOCK_SOURCE. These two socket options take a new data structure as an argument: ip_mreq_source. This is defined as

```
struct ip_mreq_source {
  struct in_addr imr_multiaddr;  /* IP multicast addr of group */
  struct in_addr imr_sourceaddr; /* IP address of source */
  struct in_addr imr_interface;  /* local IP addr of interface */
};
```

Here is sample code to block and unblock a membership.

```
struct ip_mreq_source mc_req_src;

/* construct a multicast src request structure */
mc_req_src.imr_multiaddr.s_addr  = inet_addr("232.1.1.1");
mc_req_src.imr_sourceaddr.s_addr = inet_addr("192.111.52.12");
mc_req_src.imr_interface.s_addr  = htonl(INADDR_ANY);

/* filter 192.111.52.12's packets from this group */
if ((setsockopt(sock, IPPROTO_IP, IP_BLOCK_SOURCE,
    (void*) &mc_req_src, sizeof(mc_req_src))) < 0) {
  perror("setsockopt() failed");
  exit(1);
}

/* add 192.111.52.12 back to the group */
if ((setsockopt(sock, IPPROTO_IP, IP_UNBLOCK_SOURCE,
    (void*) &mc_req_src, sizeof(mc_req_src))) < 0) {
  perror("setsockopt() failed");
  exit(1);
}
```

In controlled-source mode, all sources are denied by default and then can be individually added or removed. The add and drop of sources in controlled-source mode is achieved through the use of two more socket options. They are IP_ADD_SOURCE_MEMBERSHIP and IP_DROP_SOURCE_MEMBERSHIP. Both of these options use the same ip_mcast_source_req structure that the blocking options use. Here is sample code to add and drop memberships.

```
struct ip_mreq_source mc_req_src;

/* construct a mc src request structure */
mc_req_src.imr_multiaddr.s_addr  = inet_addr("232.1.1.1");
mc_req_src.imr_sourceaddr.s_addr = inet_addr("192.111.52.12");
mc_req_src.imr_interface.s_addr  = htonl(INADDR_ANY);

/* add 192.111.52.12 as a group source */
if ((setsockopt(sock, IPPROTO_IP, IP_ADD_SOURCE_MEMBERSHIP,
      (void*) &mc_req_src, sizeof(mc_req_src))) < 0) {
  perror("setsockopt() failed");
  exit(1);
}

/* drop 192.111.52.12 as a group source */
if ((setsockopt(sock, IPPROTO_IP, IP_DROP_SOURCE_MEMBERSHIP,
      (void*) &mc_req_src, sizeof(mc_req_src))) < 0) {
  perror("setsockopt() failed");
  exit(1);
}
```

The following errors may result when using these four new socket options:

Error	Meaning
EADDRNOTAVAIL	Address not available. When blocking an already blocked source or dropping an unjoined group.
EINVAL	Invalid. When trying a controlled-source option on an any-source group or vice versa.
EOPNOTSUPP	Operation not supported. When trying to use getsockopt() with any of these socket options.
ENOBUFS	No buffer space. Maximum number of sources that can be specified has been exceeded.

Advanced (Full-State) API

The advanced API is referred to as a full-state API because an entire set of allowed source IPs can be specified with a single call. The advanced API is implemented with the ioctl() function. The ioctl() function is used as a sort of catchall function for IO-related calls that do not fit cleanly into any other set of functions.

The implementation of ioctl() tends to vary from system to system, so the local system details on how to call it should be checked. However, the basic format is

```
#include <sys/ioctl.h>

int ioctl(int d, unsigned long request, ...)
```

The first argument is a descriptor, in this case, a socket descriptor. The second argument is the request name, defined as a constant by header values. The third argument is usually a char *argp, or a pointer to a character string argument.

For purposes of multicast source control, there are two new constants for use with ioctl(). They are SIOCGIPMSFILTER (Socket IO Control Get IP Multicast Source FILTER) and SIOCSIPMSFILTER (Socket IO Control Set IP Multicast Source FILTER). The source filter argument is the ip_msfilter structure, which is defined as

```
struct ip_msfilter {
    struct in_addr imsf_multiaddr;  /* IP multicast addr of group */
    struct in_addr imsf_interface;  /* local IP addr of interface */
    unsigned int   imsf_fmode;      /* filter mode */
    unsigned int   imsf_numsrc;     /* # of sources in src_list */
    struct in_addr imsf_slist[1];   /* start of source list */
};
```

The fields in this structure are populated as follows:

- imsf_multiaddr: The multicast address of the group

- imsf_interface: The local interface on which the group is being received

- imsf_fmode: Either MCAST_INCLUDE for any-source mode or MCAST_EXCLUDE for controlled-source mode

- imsf_numsrc: The number of sources being passed to either include or exclude

- imsf_slist[1]: The start of an array of in_addr structures containing the sources to be included or excluded

One thing to be wary of is that the imsf_fmode field is the filter mode, not the instruction specifying whether to include or exclude. This means that when the filter mode is set to MCAST_INCLUDE, it indicates any-source mode, and the source IPs passed are to be *excluded* (blocked). Similarly, when the filter mode is set to MCAST_EXCLUDE, it indicates controlled-source mode, and the source IPs passed are to be *included* (added). Here is sample code to set controlled-source SSM and add two sources.

```
struct ip_msfilter mc_filter;
struct in_addr *src_list;

/* construct a source filter request structure */
mc_filter.imsf_multiaddr.s_addr  = inet_addr("232.1.1.1");
mc_filter.imsf_interface.s_addr = htonl(INADDR_ANY);
mc_filter.imsf_fmode = MCAST_EXCLUDE;
mc_filter.imsf_numsrc = 2;
src_list = malloc(sizeof(struct in_addr)*2);
```

```
srclist[0].s_addr = inet_addr("192.111.52.11");
srclist[1].s_addr = inet_addr("192.111.52.12");
mc_filter.imsf_slist = src_list;

/* call ioctl to set mode and sources */
if (ioctl(sock, SIOCSIPMSFILTER, &mc_filter) < 0) {
  perror("ioctl() failed");
  exit(1);
}
```

The call to `ioctl()` with the set option will supersede any prior call, so to omit one of the IPs the call should be repeated with one less source IP in the list. This also allows an application to toggle between filter modes, a function that is not possible with the delta API.

5.4.2   SSM with .NET

Microsoft's .NET library includes some basic support for SSM. Specifically, the .NET Socket class contains the following four socket options:

- `AddSourceMembership`
- `DropSourceMembership`
- `BlockSource`
- `UnblockSource`

At the time this book was written, the .NET libraries were still in beta 2, and the implementation of these socket options was not functional. However, when .NET is out of beta, the functions should work something like what we next describe in these C# examples.

Assuming a `Socket` instance has already been created and bound and membership in a multicast group added, one or more sources from an any-source list could be blocked using the following code:

```
// create an IPAddress instance of your desired source IP:
IPAddress srcIP = IPAddress.Parse("192.111.52.12");

// add source membership
sock.SetSocketOption(SocketOptionLevel.IP,
                     SocketOptionName.BlockSource,
                     srcIP);
```

To stop blocking that source, the source can be re-added with this code:

```
// add source membership
sock.SetSocketOption(SocketOptionLevel.IP,
                     SocketOptionName.UnblockSource,
                     srcIP);
```

Assuming a Socket instance has already been created and bound, and membership added in a multicast group, one or more sources can be added to a controlled-source with this code:

```
// create an IPAddress instance of your desired source IP:
IPAddress srcIP = IPAddress.Parse("192.111.52.12");
```

```
// add source membership
sock.SetSocketOption(SocketOptionLevel.IP,
                     SocketOptionName.AddSourceMembership,
                     srcIP);
```

When this source is no longer needed, it can be dropped with this code:

```
// drop source membership
sock.SetSocketOption(SocketOptionLevel.IP,
                     SocketOptionName.DropSourceMembership,
                     srcIP);
```

The .NET API does not allow the equivalent of setting a "multicast filter" with multiple sources at once.

5.5 Exercises

1. For SSM, it is assumed that all sources for a particular group are known to all participants. What mechanisms can you think of to ensure this is true? How does this change if the sources are dynamic instead of static?

2. SSM greatly reduces the amount of infrastructure required to multicast across domains. What implications do you think this will have for inter-domain multicast in the future? What problems still exist?

3. Why is it important to have different, nonoverlapping address ranges for ASM and SSM?

chapter **6**

Multicast Addressing and Scoping

Until now, we have focused on the syntax of how to program multicast sockets. However, in a couple of key instances, we have glossed over the details of the semantics of some of the key parameters. In particular, these parameters include the multicast group address and port and the Time-To-Live (TTL). Obviously, choosing an address is key to avoiding collisions with other multicast groups. And setting the TTL, along with setting the address, is a key part to *scoping* the multicast group. These two features are described in this chapter.

6.1   Scoping

There are two ways to control the scope of packets sent via a multicast socket. The first is to set the Time-To-Live (TTL) to a small value. The second is to use *administrative* scoping to limit multicast packets to a part of the network with boundaries configured by a network administrator. Each of these two options is described next.

6.1.1   TTL Scoping

TTL Scoping Background

The need for and use of TTL scoping was largely motivated by the kinds of multicast routing protocols that were first developed. These protocols were based on *broadcasting* data to the entire network and then having uninterested receivers prune their links from the tree. The two most common of these protocols were the Distance Vector Multicast Routing Protocol (DVMRP) [37] and Protocol Independent Multicast-Dense Mode (PIM-DM) [1]. The details of how these protocols worked are really only of historical importance, and so instead of describing their operation here we include it in Appendix A. From an application programmer point of view, the most important thing to know is that these protocols had the undesirable property of broadcasting large amounts of data to the network. Because of this property, DVMRP and PIM-DM are referred to as dense mode or broadcast-and-prune protocols.

The approach used by dense mode protocols to get packets to all group members is obviously very unscalable. However, it was effective as a first effort in reaching potential receivers and letting them know that there was multicast traffic for a group. This function has since been replaced by using rendezvous points (or having receivers explicitly learn of sources in the SSM model). The modern set of protocols is called sparse mode or join-and-graft protocols. With these protocols, multicast packets flow only across links that have been explicitly added to a tree by join messages from receivers.

With dense mode protocols, because a potentially significant amount of unwanted traffic is being broadcast around the network, it is important to try to control the *scope* of a multicast group. The goal should be to limit the amount of unsolicited traffic that flows across links of the multicast infrastructure. Imagine the early days of multicast when the number of events was increasing rapidly. As more events were occurring, multicast-capable routers were spending an increasing amount of time removing themselves from broadcast trees because they had no interested downstream receivers. As use of multicast grew, it became increasingly important to control the scope in order to limit the areas of the network in which a broadcast from a particular source would reach. While there might still be "global" events, many more multicast groups were being created for more regional or local videoconferences. The solution was to try to control the scope of a group based on the group creator's perceived level of local, regional, or global interest.

TTL Scoping Details

Scoping is implemented by overloading the TTL function in the IP header. Consider what happens in the simple case when the TTL value of a multicast packet is set to 1. The packet makes it to the first hop router and is discarded. All receivers that are within one hop receive the packet, but no one else does. Given that the TTL can be any integer between 0 and 255, this gives a programmer a reasonable amount of control in scoping a stream of multicast packets.

Instead of re-presenting the details on how to set the TTL value of a packet, we refer you to the details in Chapters 2–4 on how to set the TTL. The more important question for the programmer is what to set the TTL value to be.

Implications of TTL Scoping

The use of TTL scoping is no longer particularly needed or particularly effective at controlling the scope of a multicast transmission. The key reason is that dense mode protocols have almost completely disappeared. Therefore, network administrators do not necessarily need to worry about overwhelming amounts of unrequested multicast traffic. TTL scoping is also not particularly effective because it presumes the use of *thresholds*. Thresholds allow a network administrator to configure routers to throw multicast packets away if their TTL value is below some level. This allows the administrator to protect a network from external multicast traffic that does not have a large enough TTL. However, in practice, because TTL scoping is not used, neither are thresholds.

Thresholds are used to keep multicast group traffic limited to a specific area. These areas can be either local, organizational, regional, or worldwide. When multicast was first being deployed, it was common practice to use 1, 16, 63, and 127, representing local subnet, organization, regional, and global, respectively. In this way, if an organization wanted to use

TTL scoping to limit transmissions from being sent outside the organization, a TTL of 16 could be used. This would be enforced by all border routers implementing a threshold for multicast. If a multicast packet was received with a TTL less than 16, it would be thrown away. In this way an application programmer could ensure that a TTL of 16 was sufficiently high to reach all receivers in the organization but not so high that packets would leak across the organization's link to the Internet. Network administrators would figure the threshold based on a value slightly higher than the diameter of their network.

Aside from the fact that TTL scoping is not particularly necessary for wide-area applications, it still has its uses for local testing. For example, if writing and testing an application, it is helpful to use a small TTL to avoid packets being sent to places they should not be due to some network configuration error. However, because proper TTL scoping sometimes requires thresholds in key places and these thresholds may not always exist, an application programmer should be careful not to create a dependency that breaks the application if the network is configured in some way that is different from that expected.

One noteworthy side effect of using TTL scoping is that Internet Control Message Protocol (ICMP) TTL-expired messages need to be suppressed for multicast. While TTLs reaching zero is an error condition for unicast packets, it is not for multicast. This is not something most programmers need to worry about, but it does have interesting implications for how a multicast version of traceroute should work.

6.1.2 Administrative Scoping

We now turn our attention to administrative scoping. Administrative scoping can be used in addition to, or instead of, TTL scoping. Whereas the TTL scoping mechanism is based on setting the TTL, administrative scoping uses the group address to control the reach of packets.

Administrative Scoping Background

Administrative scoping was created in response to the weaknesses of TTL scoping, specifically overloading a function of the IP header to limit delivery of packets and provide privacy. Also, in dense mode protocols, expiring packets could interfere with the prune process. As with other protocol details, we leave discussion of this topic to Appendix A.

Instead of overloading the TTL to control the scope of a multicast group, the group address is used to carry semantics about scoping. The idea is that some groups should be local and some should be regional. This is similar to the concept of "private" unicast IP addresses like the 10.0.0.0/8 range. A range of multicast addresses is set aside to be designated specifically to carry this semantic information. The specific ranges are described next.

Administrative Scoping Details

Administratively scoped addresses are described and discussed in IETF RFC 2365 [26]. There are several specific ranges of addresses with specific semantics, and then other ranges whose meanings are left to the discretion of the network administrator. The following is a list of these ranges:

- *239.255/16 (239.255.0.0–239.255.255.255):* This is the local scope range. It is the scope defined to have the smallest range. The locally scoped range should not overlap any other range and must be fully enclosed within any larger scope. RFC 2365 also states that if 239.255.0.0/16 becomes fully utilized, an organization can expand the local scope "downward" (can extend it to include 239.254/16, 239.253/16, etc.).

■ *239.192/16 (239.192.0.0–239.192.255.255):* This is the organization local scope. All the addresses in this space can be used by each organization. This also means that an organization can subdivide and allocate blocks of addresses by whatever means it likes. Like the local scope, the organization scope can be expanded downward. The ranges 239.0/10, 239.64/10, and 239.128/10 can be used.

■ *224.0.0/24 (224.0.0.0–224.0.0.255):* This is the link local scope. This range is obviously not in the 239.0.0.0/8 range because it was created before additional levels of administratively scoped addresses were needed and subsequently created. Link local addresses should never be routed. The behavior is similar to setting the TTL of a packet to 1. Also, it is highly unlikely that an application programmer will ever have a reason to use an address in this range.

■ *Globally scoped addresses:* Much of the rest of the address space is globally scoped. There are no specific limitations on the scope of these addresses. We will talk more about how the 224.0.0.0/4 address space is organized in the next section.

Understanding what the scoping rules are and how an organization might choose to administer its address space is critical to an application programmer since it has implications for how a programmer should choose a multicast address to use in an application. The short answer is that someone writing a simple application should use addresses from the local or organization scoped ranges. More formal, commercial applications will need to address additional considerations. These considerations are discussed in the next section.

Implications of Administrative Scoping

From a programmer's point of view, there is really no good way to determine whether a particular network implements any administrative scoping. Two ways to determine this information are to ask the network administrator or to pick an address and test the reachability to other group members (see Chapter 7).

One of the benefits of using administratively scoped addresses is that it is much easier to avoid address collisions. If a globally scoped address is needed, it becomes important to make sure no other application is using the same address. Using a locally scoped address means that checking to see if anyone is using the address is much simpler. Therefore, picking an address with a small, local scope will make building a service on top of multicast much easier.

6.2 Multicast Address Space

The multicast address space is not like any other part of the IP address space. This means that multicast addresses are not allocated in blocks by the Internet Assigned Numbers Authority (IANA). The entire space is either reserved, assigned for specific applications, or statistically assigned to autonomous systems (ASs) and subnetworks. The analogy for unicast would be

Table 6.1 Multicast address space categories.

Address Range	CIDR Block	Description
224.0.0.0–224.0.0.255	(224.0.0.0/24)	Local Network Control Block
224.0.1.0–224.0.1.255	(224.0.1.0/24)	Internetwork Control Block
224.0.2.0–224.0.255.0		AD-HOC Block
224.1.0.0–224.1.255.255	(224.1.0.0/16)	ST Multicast Groups
224.2.0.0–224.2.255.255	(224.2.0.0/16)	SDP/SAP Block
224.3.0.0–231.255.255.255		RESERVED
232.0.0.0–232.255.255.255	(232.0.0.0/8)	Source Specific Multicast Block
233.0.0.0–233.255.255.255	(233.0.0.0/8)	GLOP Block
234.0.0.0–238.255.255.255		RESERVED
239.0.0.0–239.255.255.255	(239.0.0.0/8)	Administratively Scoped Block

that *all* IP addresses for *all* hosts are assigned using a protocol like the Dynamic Host Configuration Protocol (DHCP). Imagine the challenge of requiring every user of the Internet to go to a central server to temporarily obtain an IP address. While there are certainly benefits, the overhead would likely be prohibitive. To carry the analogy further, the administrative scoped range discussed in the previous section is like the private unicast address spaces 10/8 and 192.168/16. Therefore, finding an address to use for a multicast application is a nontrivial exercise.

The Internet Engineering Task Force (IETF) has developed a request for comments (RFC) to provide guidance on how application programmers and network administrators should use the Class D multicast addresses. RFC 3171 describes how the multicast address space is divided [2]. The basic groups are as in Table 6.1. For specific information on each of these ranges, see RFC 3171. The ranges most likely to be used by an application programmer are 224.2/16, 232/8, 233/8, and 239/8. The 239/8 range was described in the previous section.

The 224.2/16 range is used by the session directory (*sdr*) tool. *Sdr* periodically sends announcements [21] for sessions it creates [22] to a well-known multicast address. Therefore, a user running *sdr* can see a list of most, if not all, sessions. *Sdr* also assists users in creating sessions. Part of this process consists of *sdr* choosing a random address not already in use. Because *sdr* is advertising this session, a user can use this address for as long as the session is actively being advertised. Collisions may still occur but are much less likely. This process was created and used as part of the original multicast backbone. While it works well for certain kinds of applications, it does not necessarily work in the case when an application wants to choose a single address and use it forever. However, given that the address space is scarce, according to RFC 3171, IANA is unlikely to allocate even a single address to a specific application. The multicast community expects that applications either will be able to accept as input the multicast address to use or will be able to randomly choose from a block of addresses and deal with rechoosing if there is a conflict.

The 232/8 range is for SSM. SSM was described in Chapter 5. What is nice about the SSM range is that the IP source address together with the group address uniquely identifies the multicast group (called a channel in SSM terminology). This means that each IP address can use the full 232/8 address range without colliding with any other host. Obviously, collisions can still occur if there are multiple multicast applications running on the same host, but even in this case the probability is very small.

The 233/8 range is for "GLOP" range. GLOP is not an acronym but rather refers to the allocation of a group of addresses to each autonomous system. Of the 32 bits, the first 8 are 233, the next 16 are for the 16-bit AS number, and the final 8 represent the 256 groups assigned to the AS. The encoding of the AS number into the middle 16 bits is straightforward and is described in RFC 2770 [28]. The GLOP range is typically used for organizations that have their own AS and want to statically assign multicast groups for particular content. Access to these addresses is typically not available to most users. The idea is that if a company like CNN wanted to broadcast a video feed, it would get an address from the GLOP block assigned to its AS. This way, it could advertise the address on a Web page. However, this application is an example better suited for SSM. And so, as SSM becomes more popular, it is expected that these kinds of single/static source applications will migrate to using SSM and its address range.

The IETF is also considering other proposals. For example, one proposal suggests using an address range like 225/8 and appending the network prefix. For example, UC–Santa Barbara would be able to use the address range 224.128.111.0/24 because its unicast address space is 128.111/16. Obviously, an organization with a /24 would have access to only one multicast address, and any organization with fewer addresses than a /24 would have no multicast addresses. But at least this solution has the advantage of avoiding the indirect association between the AS number and the multicast address space. RFC 3171 continues to be the most up-to-date source of information for how the 224/4 address range is allocated.

6.3   Selecting a Multicast Address

In several places in this chapter, we have referred to how to select a multicast address. From the length of the various sections, it should be obvious that choosing a multicast address is not always straightforward.

Selecting a multicast address *is* straightforward if the application being developed is for use by only a few people. Examples of these kinds of applications include something written as part of a class assignment, some private conferencing tool, an experiment by someone just learning multicast, and so on. In these cases, the application writer can hard-code an address from the 239.255/16 range. If the application is running across inter-domain boundaries, the right thing to do is to contact the network administrator. However, many users consider this more trouble than it is worth. While we certainly advocate following the right procedure, probably the least damaging, unofficial solution for a quick test is just to pick something random from the 224.2/16 range. Finally, as SSM becomes more widely deployed, application programmers who build applications based on SSM will need to use the 232/8 address range.

Selecting a multicast address for a more widely deployed application is more difficult. In almost all cases, the application programmer should be prepared to handle dynamic addresses. Unless there is a clear reason, IANA will not assign specific addresses to specific applications.

Therefore, applications that will be widely deployed and used should not have hard-coded addresses. Often, an application programmer can leave the selection of an address to the user. Users can be expected to be allocated an address from a network administrator or some other "owner" of a set of addresses.

One final fact to keep in mind when programming and testing applications is that different addresses in the Class D address space have different semantics and are handled differently by the network. While this should be obvious for anyone who has read this chapter and/or reviewed the relevant RFCs, the point is still worth making. An application might work with a 239.255/16 address but not with a 192.255.255/24 address. Therefore, application programmers need to be extremely careful in programming applications to find the right address for the application. It is also important that application programmers not necessarily assume that multicast connectivity exists for all interested receivers. This is a topic addressed in the next two chapters.

6.4 Java Multicast Address Scope Methods

Almost all the syntax with regard to scoping and addressing in C, Java, and .NET has already been presented. However, one additional set of functions is available in Java. Starting in Java 2 v1.4, a number of addressing-specific APIs for multicast have been added to the `InetAddress` class. These are simple boolean methods to check if the `InetAddress` instance is in a particular multicast scope.

`java.net.InetAddress` methods (Java 2 v1.4 or higher):

```
public boolean isMCGlobal()
public boolean isMCLinkLocal()
public boolean isMCSiteLocal()
public boolean isMCOrgLocal()
```

These are utility routines to check if the multicast address has global scope, link scope, site scope, or organization scope, respectively. These methods return true or false based on the following hard-coded constants:

- isMCGlobal(): Returns true for address range 224.0.1.0–238.255.255.255

- isMCLinkLocal(): Returns true for address range 224.0.0/24 (224.0.0.0–224.0.0.255)

- isMCSiteLocal(): Returns true for address range 239.255/16 (239.255.0.0–239.255.255.255)

- isMCOrgLocal(): Returns true for address range 239.192.0.0–239.192.255.255

  For example,

  ```
  InetAddress addr;
  try {
    addr = InetAddress.getByName("239.255.10.10");
  ```

```
} catch (UnknownHostException e) {
  e.printStackTrace();
}
if (addr.isMCGlobal())
  System.out.println("This address is a global multicast address.");
```

These methods provide a programmatic way to test the scope of a multicast address. They can be called on nonmulticast addresses as well, but they will simply return false.

6.5 Exercises

1. What are the options available for an enterprise to allocate addresses in the organization local administratively scoped range?

2. How does TTL scoping cause prune problems with dense mode protocols?

3. What happens if two groups use the same multicast group address?

4. What happens if, in addition to the multicast group address, two applications also use the same port number?

5. How do IP multicast addresses translate into MAC addresses for a protocol like Ethernet?

6. What reasons prohibit multicast addresses from being allocated in the same manner as unicast IP addresses?

7. How are collisions avoided for the same group address in SSM?

8. How might an application user go about finding and using a GLOP address?

chapter **7**

Multicast Reachability and Scalability

At this point, we have covered about 99% of what an application programmer needs to know in order to get an application to open a multicast socket and either send or receive. However, writing a multicast-based application is not always a simple matter of sending and receiving as it can be with unicast. Therefore, in this and the next chapter, we address several key issues that application programmers should be aware of and offer some code that may be of use in various situations.

In this chapter, we focus on reachability and scalability. The two go hand in hand because evaluating reachability demands consideration for scalability. Reachability for unicast is typically just assumed. For multicast, not only is connectivity (and, subsequently, reachability) questionable—primarily because of a lack of deployment—but testing whether all a group's receivers can be reached by a source adds a whole new dimension of complexity. Therefore, in this chapter, we attempt to give you an awareness of the potential problems and the tools to solve them.

7.1 Multicast Reachability

With unicast, reachability is fairly simple to test. The most basic aliveness test across a network is to use the ping program from one host to another.

```
$ ping 192.115.102.78
PING 192.115.102.78 (192.115.102.78): 56 data bytes
64 bytes from 192.115.102.78: icmp_seq=0 ttl=239 time=16.997 ms
64 bytes from 192.115.102.78: icmp_seq=1 ttl=239 time=17.101 ms
^C
--- 192.115.102.78 ping statistics ---
2 packets transmitted, 2 packets received, 0% packet loss
round-trip min/avg/max/stddev = 16.997/17.049/17.101/0.052 ms
```

Under the hood, the ping program sends Internet Control Message Protocol (ICMP) packets. The message sent is an ECHO_REQUEST datagram, which, when received by the destination host, elicits an ECHO_RESPONSE. The echo response data is then displayed for the end user. Some systems report detailed statistics by default, whereas other systems simply indicate the presence or absense of a response.

```
% ping 192.115.102.78
192.115.102.78 is alive

% ping 192.1.1.1
192.1.1.1 is unreachable
```

On some operating systems (most notably BSD systems), the ping program can be used to get some very specific multicast results [34]. Recall from Chapter 6 reserved multicast addresses 224.0.0.1 (the all-hosts group) and 224.0.0.2 (the all-routers group). All multicast-enabled hosts and routers are required to join these multicast groups, respectively, which allows them to respond to a ping on that group address. Using ping on the all-routers group elicits a response from all multicast-enabled routers on the subnet.

```
$ ping 224.0.0.2
PING 224.0.0.2 (224.0.0.2): 56 data bytes
64 bytes from 192.111.2.32: icmp_seq=0 ttl=62 time=0.356 ms
64 bytes from 192.111.2.32: icmp_seq=1 ttl=62 time=0.764 ms
^C
--- 224.0.0.2 ping statistics ---
2 packets transmitted, 2 packets received, 0% packet loss
round-trip min/avg/max/stddev = 0.356/0.560/0.764/0.204 ms
```

Because there was only one multicast-enabled router on this subnet, this looks very much like a normal unicast ping (other than the fact that we specified a multicast address instead of a host IP). However, if you ping the all-hosts group, you will get a response from every host on the subnet.

```
$ ping 224.0.0.1
PING 224.0.0.1 (224.0.0.1): 56 data bytes
64 bytes from 192.111.52.18: icmp_seq=0 ttl=255 time=0.226 ms
64 bytes from 192.111.52.24: icmp_seq=0 ttl=255 time=0.261 ms (DUP!)
64 bytes from 192.111.52.19: icmp_seq=0 ttl=255 time=0.267 ms (DUP!)
64 bytes from 192.111.52.31: icmp_seq=0 ttl=255 time=0.272 ms (DUP!)
64 bytes from 192.111.52.30: icmp_seq=0 ttl=255 time=0.277 ms (DUP!)
64 bytes from 192.111.52.15: icmp_seq=0 ttl=255 time=0.283 ms (DUP!)
64 bytes from 192.111.52.12: icmp_seq=0 ttl=255 time=0.300 ms (DUP!)
64 bytes from 192.111.52.29: icmp_seq=0 ttl=255 time=0.306 ms (DUP!)
64 bytes from 192.111.52.11: icmp_seq=0 ttl=255 time=0.312 ms (DUP!)
64 bytes from 192.111.52.10: icmp_seq=0 ttl=255 time=0.317 ms (DUP!)
64 bytes from 192.111.52.32: icmp_seq=0 ttl=255 time=0.323 ms (DUP!)
64 bytes from 192.111.52.25: icmp_seq=0 ttl=255 time=0.590 ms (DUP!)
64 bytes from 192.111.2.32: icmp_seq=0 ttl=62 time=1.629 ms (DUP!)
64 bytes from 192.111.52.1: icmp_seq=0 ttl=64 time=2.012 ms (DUP!)
64 bytes from 192.111.52.241: icmp_seq=0 ttl=64 time=6.287 ms (DUP!)
^C
```

```
--- 224.0.0.1 ping statistics ---
1 packets transmitted, 1 packets received, +14 duplicates, 0% packet loss
round-trip min/avg/max/stddev = 0.226/0.911/6.287/1.528 ms
```

In this example, even though only 1 ping packet was sent, 15 packets were received, 1 each from 15 different hosts (which ping somewhat misleadingly identified as 1 packet and 14 duplicates). While this capability has its uses, it has a number of severe drawbacks.

- Many operating systems' versions of ping do not support multicast pings.

- ping will support only pinging the all-routers and all-hosts groups, so this does not allow testing against an arbitrary multicast address.

- Traffic sent to all-routers or all-hosts multicast groups is restricted to the local subnet and is never routed.

These restrictions greatly limit the utility of the existing ping program in multicast reachability testing.

When sending a unicast ping, the expectation is that one response will be heard for each ping. As is evident from the example, there may be any number of responses to a multicast ping. Because the multicast service model does not provide for groupwide knowledge of receivers, there is no way to know how many receivers should respond. The best analogy is the often repeated joke from a lecturer: "Anyone in the back of the room who cannot hear me should raise their hand." Not receiving a ping to a multicast group is an important failure, but one that will go unnoticed because the host requesting the ping will never know that an unreachable host did not respond.

If a host issuing a multicast ping does not know how many receivers there are, problems of scalability are also created. Theoretically, the number of ping responses could range from 0 to every single host in the entire Internet. Imagine what would happen if every host on the Internet sent one datagram to a single Internet host at the same time. Not only would the host melt down under the load of the traffic, but so would many of the routers and switches near the host.

Obviously, it is highly unlikely that a group exists, or will ever exist, that consists of every host on the Internet. However, the scalability implications are obvious. For this reason, there is no widely used multicast ping program. Additional logistics, such as the fact that not every host on the Internet has multicast connectivity to every other host and Network Address Translation (NAT) and firewalls would block many packets, make this scenario infeasible as well.

The primary point, however, is that the scalability problem exposed by a multicast ping is not unique to ping only. All multicast-enabled programs that expect any type of feedback, often called many to one, need to deal with scalability issues created by large group sizes. This chapter will walk through the creation of an application-level multicast ping program. We will then examine some mechanisms to scale the responses and how these techniques can be applied more generally.

7.2 Multicast Ping

In this section, we will discuss the creation of mping, an application-level multicast ping program written in C. By running mping receivers or listeners on multiple hosts, mping can be used to get ping-like statistics and responses from all the receivers within range. The mping program can be run on any arbitrary multicast address, which will allow its packets to be routable across multicast-enabled routers, switches, and tunnels.

To start with, the following is the listing of mping.h, the mping header file. This file defines some basic constants, the structure of the mping packet, and function prototypes.

mping.h

```
 1   #include <sys/types.h>  /* for type definitions */
 2   #include <sys/socket.h> /* for socket calls */
 3   #include <netinet/in.h> /* for address structs */
 4   #include <arpa/inet.h>  /* for sockaddr_in */
 5   #include <unistd.h>     /* for symbolic constants */
 6   #include <errno.h>      /* for system error messages */
 7   #include <sys/time.h>   /* for timeval and gettimeofday */
 8   #include <netdb.h>      /* for hostname calls */
 9   #include <signal.h>     /* for signal calls */
10   #include <stdlib.h>     /* for close and getopt calls */
11   #include <stdio.h>      /* for printf and fprintf */
12
13   #define MAX_BUF_LEN       1024   /* size of receive buffer */
14   #define MAX_HOSTNAME_LEN  256    /* size of host name buffer */
15   #define MAX_PINGS           5    /* number of pings to send */
16
17   #define VERSION_MAJOR 1   /* mping version major */
18   #define VERSION_MINOR 0   /* mping version minor */
19
20   #define SENDER   's'      /* mping sender identifier */
21   #define RECEIVER 'r'      /* mping receiver identifier */
22
23   /* mping packet structure */
24   struct mping_struct {
25     unsigned short version_major;
26     unsigned short version_minor;
27     unsigned char  type;
28     unsigned char  ttl;
29     struct in_addr src_host;
30     struct in_addr dest_host;
31     unsigned int   seq_no;
32     pid_t          pid;
33     struct timeval tv;
34   } mping_packet;
35
36   /* pointer to mping packet buffer */
37   struct mping_struct *rcvd_pkt;
38
```

```
39  int sock;    /* socket descriptor */
40  pid_t pid;   /* pid of mping program */
41
42  struct sockaddr_in mc_addr;     /* socket address structure */
43  struct ip_mreq    mc_request; /* multicast request structure */
44
45  struct in_addr localIP;         /* address struct for local IP */
46
47  /* counters and statistics variables */
48  int     packets_sent = 0;
49  int     packets_rcvd = 0;
50  double rtt_total     = 0;
51  double rtt_max       = 0;
52  double rtt_min       = 999999999.0;
53
54  /* default command-line arguments */
55  char          arg_mcaddr_str[16] = "239.255.255.1";
56  int           arg_mcport          = 10000;
57  unsigned char arg_ttl             = 1;
58
59  int verbose=0;
60
61  /* function prototypes */
62  void init_socket();
63  void get_local_host_info();
64  void send_mping();
65  void send_packet(struct mping_struct *packet);
66  void sender_listen_loop();
67  void receiver_listen_loop();
68  void subtract_timeval(struct timeval *val,
69                        const struct timeval *sub);
70  double timeval_to_ms(const struct timeval *val);
71  int  process_mping_packet(char *packet, int recv_len,
72                        unsigned char type);
73  void clean_exit();
74  void usage();
```

mping.h

The mping_packet structure is defined in lines 23–34. The structure contains the minimum information we need to transmit in order to keep the packets small. A version number with a major and minor component ensures that if we modify mping to an incompatible version (as we will do later in this chapter), we can either ignore packets that do not match the version or build in backward compatibility. A type field will indicate whether this is a sender or receiver packet. The ttl, src_host, and dest_host fields will indicate the TTL, the sourcing host, and the group address to which the ping was sent. A sequence number field is used to keep track of the ping iteration with which we are dealing. This is important since UDP does not guarantee ordering or reliable delivery of packets. A process ID, or pid number, of the mping source is used to demultiplex multiple mping senders on the same address. Finally, a timeval structure is used to record the time the packet was sent. This information is used by the receiving host to determine the round-trip time.

The following is the mping main() code:

mping.c/main()

```
1   int main(int argc, char **argv) {
2     int c;              /* hold command-line args */
3     int rcvflag=0;      /* receiver flag */
4     int sndflag=0;      /* sender flag */
5     extern int getopt(); /* for getopt */
6     extern char *optarg; /* for getopt */
7
8     /* parse command-line arguments */
9     while ((c = getopt(argc, argv, "vrsa:p:t:")) != -1) {
10      switch (c) {
11      case 'r':
12        /* mping receiver */
13        rcvflag=1;
14        break;
15      case 's':
16        /* mping sender */
17        sndflag=1;
18        break;
19      case 'v':
20        verbose=1;
21        break;
22      case 'a':
23        /* mping address override */
24        strcpy(arg_mcaddr_str, optarg);
25        break;
26      case 'p':
27        /* mping port override */
28        arg_mcport = atoi(optarg);
29        break;
30      case 't':
31        /* mping ttl override */
32        arg_ttl = atoi(optarg);
33        break;
34      case '?':
35        usage();
36        break;
37      }
38    }
```

```
39
40    /* verify one and only one send or receive flag */
41    if ( ((!rcvflag) && (!sndflag)) ||
42         ((rcvflag) && (sndflag)) ) {
43      usage();
44    }
45
46    printf("mping version %d.%d\n", VERSION_MAJOR, VERSION_MINOR);
47
48    init_socket();
49
50    get_local_host_info();
51
52    if (sndflag) {
53      printf("mpinging %s/%d with ttl=%d:\n\n",
54              arg_mcaddr_str, arg_mcport, arg_ttl);
55
56      /* catch interrupts with clean_exit() */
57      signal(SIGINT, clean_exit);
58
59      /* catch alarm signal with send_mping() */
60      signal(SIGALRM, send_mping);
61
62      /* send an alarm signal now */
63      send_mping(SIGALRM);
64
65      /* listen for response packets */
66      sender_listen_loop();
67
68    } else {
69      receiver_listen_loop();
70    }
71    exit(0);
72  }
```

mping.c/main()

The main() function first parses the command line arguments. The only required argument for mping is a sender (–s) or receiver (–r) flag. Optional arguments include verbose mode (–v) and overriding the default values: address (–a address), port (–p port), and TTL (–t ttl). If any of the arguments are incorrect, a usage message is output according to the following code:

mping.c/usage()

```
1  void usage() {
2    printf("Usage: mping -r|-s [-v] [-a address]");
```

```
 3     printf(" [-p port] [-t ttl]\n\n");
 4     printf("-r|-s        Receiver or sender. Required argument,\n");
 5     printf("             mutually exclusive\n");
 6     printf("-a address   Multicast address to listen/send on,\n");
 7     printf("             overrides the default.\n");
 8     printf("-p port      Multicast port to listen/send on,\n");
 9     printf("             overrides the default of 10000.\n");
10     printf("-p ttl       Multicast time to live to send,\n");
11     printf("             overrides the default of 1.\n");
12     printf("-v           Verbose mode\n");
13     exit(1);
14  }
```

mping.c/usage()

Once the arguments are parsed, the function init_socket() is called to initialize the socket. The get_local_host_info() function is called to store local host data such as the IP address and pid used to populate the mping packets.

Back in the main() function, lines 52–66 show the high-level code operation for mping senders. First, the mping send information is displayed to the user. Then signal handling is used to execute the clean_exit() function when an interrupt occurs. This will display final statistics when the program is terminated with a Control-C. Next, we catch the alarm signal with the function send_mping(). The alarm is used to run this function once per second, generating mping send packets each time while listening for responses the rest of the time. Next, we send our first mping packet by generating an alarm signal. Once we return from sending the packet, we call sender_listen_loop() to loop listening for response packets to our mping, using the alarm signal at one-second intervals to send additional packets.

If mping is being run as a receiver, the function receiver_listen_loop() is called. As a receiver, the program will loop indefinitely, listening and responding to mping send packets.

Now that we have presented the flow of the high-level program, we present the details of the individual functions. The first is the init_socket() function.

mping.c/init_socket()

```
1  void init_socket() {
2    int flag_on=1;
3
4    /* create a UDP socket */
5    if ((sock = socket(AF_INET, SOCK_DGRAM, IPPROTO_UDP)) < 0) {
6      perror("receive socket() failed");
7      exit(1);
8    }
9
```

```
10     /* set reuse port to on to allow multiple binds per host */
11     if ((setsockopt(sock, SOL_SOCKET, SO_REUSEADDR, &flag_on,
12         sizeof(flag_on))) < 0) {
13       perror("setsockopt() failed");
14       exit(1);
15     }
16
17     /* construct a multicast address structure */
18     memset(&mc_addr, 0, sizeof(mc_addr));
19     mc_addr.sin_family = AF_INET;
20     mc_addr.sin_addr.s_addr = inet_addr(arg_mcaddr_str);
21     mc_addr.sin_port = htons(arg_mcport);
22
23     /* bind multicast address to socket */
24     if ((bind(sock, (struct sockaddr *) &mc_addr,
25         sizeof(mc_addr))) < 0) {
26       perror("bind() failed");
27       exit(1);
28     }
29
30     /* construct an IGMP join request structure */
31     mc_request.imr_multiaddr.s_addr = inet_addr(arg_mcaddr_str);
32     mc_request.imr_interface.s_addr = htonl(INADDR_ANY);
33
34     /* send an ADD MEMBERSHIP message via setsockopt */
35     if ((setsockopt(sock, IPPROTO_IP, IP_ADD_MEMBERSHIP,
36         (void*) &mc_request, sizeof(mc_request))) < 0) {
37       perror("setsockopt() failed");
38       exit(1);
39     }
40   }
```

mping.c/init_socket()

The init_socket() function is used to set up the socket. It is generic to both the sender and receiver since the mping receiver must be able to both listen to and respond on the mping multicast address. The specific sections of code include

Lines 4–8: Create a generic UDP socket using the socket() call.

Lines 10–15: Using setsockopt(), the address reuse option is set so a user will be able to run multiple mping programs on a single host. Without setting this option, we would not be able to run an mping receiver and sender simultaneously on the same machine.

Lines 17–21: Populate the multicast address structure with the appropriate addresses, either the defaults or the overridden values from the command line.

Lines 23–28: Issue a bind() call on our socket, which is required for receiving multicast packets.

Lines 30–39: Populate the multicast request structure and use it with setsockopt() to join the multicast group.

The next function to look at is get_local_host_info(). The code is as follows:

mping.c/get_local_host_info()

```
1   void get_local_host_info() {
2     char hostname[MAX_HOSTNAME_LEN];
3     struct hostent* hostinfo;
4
5     /* look up local hostname */
6     gethostname(hostname, MAX_HOSTNAME_LEN);
7
8     if (verbose) printf("Localhost is %s, ", hostname);
9
10    /* use gethostbyname to get host's IP address */
11    if ((hostinfo = gethostbyname(hostname)) == NULL) {
12      perror("gethostbyname() failed");
13    }
14    localIP.s_addr = *((unsigned long *) hostinfo->h_addr_list[0]);
15
16    if (verbose) printf("%s\n", inet_ntoa(localIP));
17
18    pid = getpid();
19  }
```

mping.c/get_local_host_info()

The get_local_host_info() function populates local host information that is used to populate the mping packets. The local IP address is looked up by first using the gethostname() call and then using the hostname as input to the gethostbyname() call. The gethostbyname() function returns a list of IP addresses (used if the host is multihomed). In this case, we simply take the first IP address returned.

The next function to look at is send_mping(). The code is as follows:

mping.c/send_mping()

```
1   void send_mping() {
2     static int current_ping=0;
3     struct timeval now;
4
5     /* increment count, check if done */
6     if (current_ping++ >= MAX_PINGS) {
7       clean_exit();
```

```
8    }
9
10   /* clear send buffer */
11   memset(&mping_packet, 0, sizeof(mping_packet));
12
13   /* populate the mping packet */
14   mping_packet.type = SENDER;
15   mping_packet.version_major = htons(VERSION_MAJOR);
16   mping_packet.version_minor = htons(VERSION_MINOR);
17   mping_packet.seq_no = htonl(current_ping);
18   mping_packet.src_host.s_addr = localIP.s_addr;
19   mping_packet.dest_host.s_addr = inet_addr(arg_mcaddr_str);
20   mping_packet.ttl = arg_ttl;
21   mping_packet.pid = pid;
22
23   gettimeofday(&now, NULL);
24   mping_packet.tv.tv_sec  = htonl(now.tv_sec);
25   mping_packet.tv.tv_usec = htonl(now.tv_usec);
26
27   /* send the outgoing packet */
28   send_packet(&mping_packet);
29
30   /* set another alarm call to send in 1 second */
31   signal(SIGALRM, send_mping);
32   alarm(1);
33 }
```

mping.c/send_mping()

The send_mping() function is used only by mping senders and is called by the alarm signal at one-second intervals.

The first thing we do is check if we are done. The program is configured to send only MAX_PINGS packets before exiting (currently, set to 5 in mping.h). The counter current_ping is used to keep track of how many we have sent. Notice that since the function is called at one-second intervals, it is set up to wait one second before determining if it is done. This allows one second to receive any response packets before exiting the program.

In lines 10–25, the mping packet is initialized and populated. The packet type is a SENDER, and the version information is populated from the header constants. The current_ping counter is used to populate the sequence number. The source address is the local IP address, and the destination address is the multicast group address. The pid is the process ID of the local mping program that is used to demultiplex responses in the case of multiple senders on the same host using the same group address. The system call gettimeofday() is used to populate the local timestamp. The send_packet() function is used to send the outgoing packet.

When a signal is caught, any previous calls to catch that signal are reset. Therefore, before we exit the function we register send_mping() to catch the next alarm signal using the signal() call. The alarm() function is used to set the next alarm for one second so this function can run again.

The next function to look at is send_packet(). The code is as follows:

mping.c/send_packet()

```
1   void send_packet(struct mping_struct *packet) {
2     int pkt_len;
3
4     pkt_len = sizeof(struct mping_struct);
5
6     /* send string to multicast address */
7     if ((sendto(sock, packet, pkt_len, 0,
8         (struct sockaddr *) &mc_addr,
9         sizeof(mc_addr))) != pkt_len) {
10     perror("sendto() sent incorrect number of bytes");
11     exit(1);
12    }
13    packets_sent++;
14  }
```

mping.c/send_packet()

The send_packet() function is generic to both mping senders and receivers. The function consists of a sendto() call on our multicast socket. This sends the contents of the global mping packet structure. A packets_sent variable is used to keep track of the sent packet count.

The next function to look at is sender_listen_loop(). The code is as follows:

mping.c/sender_listen_loop()

```
1   void sender_listen_loop() {
2     char recv_packet[MAX_BUF_LEN+1]; /* buffer to receive packet */
3     int recv_len;                    /* length of packet received */
4     struct timeval current_time;     /* time value structure */
5     double rtt;                      /* round-trip time */
6
7     while (1) {
8
9       /* clear the receive buffer */
10      memset(recv_packet, 0, sizeof(recv_packet));
11
12      /* block waiting to receive a packet */
```

```
13      if ((recv_len = recvfrom(sock, recv_packet, MAX_BUF_LEN,
14          0, NULL, 0)) < 0) {
15        if (errno == EINTR) {
16          /* interrupt is ok */
17          continue;
18        } else {
19          perror("recvfrom() failed");
20          exit(1);
21        }
22      }
23
24      /* get current time */
25      gettimeofday(&current_time, NULL);
26
27      /* process the received packet */
28      if (process_mping_packet(recv_packet, recv_len, RECEIVER) == 0) {
29
30        /* packet processed successfully */
31
32        /* calculate round-trip time in milliseconds */
33        subtract_timeval(&current_time, &rcvd_pkt->tv);
34        rtt = timeval_to_ms(&current_time);
35
36        /* keep rtt total, min and max */
37        rtt_total += rtt;
38        if (rtt > rtt_max) rtt_max = rtt;
39        if (rtt < rtt_min) rtt_min = rtt;
40
41        /* output received packet information */
42        printf("%d bytes from %s: seqno=%d ttl=%d time=%.3f ms\n",
43              recv_len, inet_ntoa(rcvd_pkt->src_host),
44              rcvd_pkt->seq_no, rcvd_pkt->ttl, rtt);
45      }
46    }
47  }
```

mping.c/sender_listen_loop()

The sender_listen_loop() function is used to loop listening for response packets to an mping. The recvfrom() call is used to listen for incoming packets on the multicast group address. Since the alarm signal used to send packets at one-second intervals will interrupt the recvfrom() call, this needs to be handled. By checking if the error code returned is equal to the system constant EINTR, the program can determine if this is an interrupt signal. If it is, the program simply continues and loops back to continue to listen for packets.

Once a packet is received, the program stores the current timestamp for calculating the round-trip time. The process_mping_packet() function is called to determine if the packet is a valid mping response for this sender and returns 0 if the packet was successfully validated. If the packet is valid, the program calculates the round-trip time by subtracting the sent time from current time and converting to milliseconds. This is done by using two functions described next, subtract_timeval() and timeval_to_ms(). The sent time is also calculated on the mping sender (passed to the recipient in the mping send packet, and returned to the sender in the mping response packet). In this way, there is no cross-host time skew to worry about.

Once the round-trip time is calculated, the total, min, and max round-trip times are stored for the final statistics. Last, the response information is output to the end user.

The subtract_timeval() and timeval_to_ms() functions are defined as follows:

mping.c/subtract_timeval()

```
1  void subtract_timeval(struct timeval *val, const struct timeval *sub) {
2    /* subtract sub from val and leave result in val */
3
4    if ((val->tv_usec -= sub->tv_usec) < 0) {
5      val->tv_sec--;
6      val->tv_usec += 1000000;
7    }
8    val->tv_sec -= sub->tv_sec;
9  }
```

mping.c/subtract_timeval()

The subtract_timeval() function takes pointers to two timeval structures as arguments. The contents of the second structure are subtracted from (and stored in) the first structure.

mping.c/timeval_to_ms()

```
1  double timeval_to_ms(const struct timeval *val) {
2    /* return the timeval converted to a number of milliseconds */
3
4    return (val->tv_sec * 1000.0 + val->tv_usec / 1000.0);
5  }
```

mping.c/timeval_to_ms()

The timeval_to_ms() function takes a timeval structure and returns the equivalent number of milliseconds in a type double.

The next function to look at is process_mping_packet(). The code is as follows:

mping.c/process_mping_packet()

```
 1  int process_mping_packet(char *packet, int recv_len,
 2                           unsigned char type) {
 3
 4    /* validate packet size */
 5    if (recv_len < sizeof(struct mping_struct)) {
 6      if (verbose) printf("Discarding packet: too small (%d)\n",
 7                          strlen(packet));
 8      return(-1);
 9    }
10
11    /* cast data to mping_struct */
12    rcvd_pkt = (struct mping_struct *) packet;
13
14    /* convert required fields to host byte order */
15    rcvd_pkt->version_major = ntohs(rcvd_pkt->version_major);
16    rcvd_pkt->version_minor = ntohs(rcvd_pkt->version_minor);
17    rcvd_pkt->seq_no        = ntohl(rcvd_pkt->seq_no);
18    rcvd_pkt->tv.tv_sec     = ntohl(rcvd_pkt->tv.tv_sec);
19    rcvd_pkt->tv.tv_usec    = ntohl(rcvd_pkt->tv.tv_usec);
20
21    /* validate mping version matches */
22    if ((rcvd_pkt->version_major != VERSION_MAJOR) ||
23        (rcvd_pkt->version_minor != VERSION_MINOR)) {
24      if (verbose) printf("Discarding packet: version mismatch (%d.%d)\n",
25                          rcvd_pkt->version_major,
26                          rcvd_pkt->version_minor);
27      return(-1);
28    }
29
30    /* validate mping packet type (sender or receiver) */
31    if (rcvd_pkt->type != type) {
32      if (verbose) {
33        switch (rcvd_pkt->type) {
34        case SENDER:
35          printf("Discarding sender packet\n");
36          break;
37        case RECEIVER:
38          printf("Discarding receiver packet\n");
39          break;
40        case '?':
41          printf("Discarding packet: unknown type(%c)\n",
42                 rcvd_pkt->type);
43          break;
44        }
45      }
```

```
46      return(-1);
47    }
48
49    /* if response packet, validate pid */
50    if (rcvd_pkt->type == RECEIVER) {
51      if (rcvd_pkt->pid != pid) {
52        if (verbose)
53          printf("Discarding packet: pid mismatch (%d/%d)\n",
54                 (int)pid, (int)rcvd_pkt->pid);
55        return(-1);
56      }
57    }
58
59    /* packet validated, increment counter */
60    packets_rcvd++;
61
62    return(0);
63  }
```

mping.c/process_mping_packet()

The process_mping_packet() function is generic to both the mping sender and the mping receiver. The function takes a pointer to the packet to be validated, and a type that is the packet type the program is expecting (SENDER or RECEIVER). This is used to filter invalid packets and packets that are not relevant: send packets for mping senders and received packets for mping receivers. If the packet is deemed valid, 0 is returned; otherwise −1 is returned.

This function checks a number of reasons to discard the packet, including invalid packet size, mismatched version number, mismatched process ID on response packets, and send packets for senders and response packets for receivers. A packets_rcvd variable is incremented for each validated packet.

The next function to look at is receiver_listen_loop(). The code is as follows:

mping.c/receiver_listen_loop()

```
1  void receiver_listen_loop() {
2    char recv_packet[MAX_BUF_LEN+1]; /* buffer to receive string */
3    int recv_len;                    /* len of string received */
4
5    printf("Listening on %s/%d:\n\n", arg_mcaddr_str, arg_mcport);
6
7    while (1) {
8
9      /* clear the receive buffer */
10     memset(recv_packet, 0, sizeof(recv_packet));
11
12     /* block waiting to receive a packet */
```

```
13      if ((recv_len = recvfrom(sock, recv_packet, MAX_BUF_LEN,
14          0, NULL, 0)) < 0) {
15        perror("recvfrom() failed");
16        exit(1);
17      }
18
19      /* process the received packet */
20      if (process_mping_packet(recv_packet, recv_len, SENDER) == 0) {
21
22        /* packet processed successfully */
23        printf("Replying to mping from %s bytes=%d seqno=%d ttl=%d\n",
24            inet_ntoa(rcvd_pkt->src_host), recv_len,
25            rcvd_pkt->seq_no, rcvd_pkt->ttl);
26
27        /* populate mping response packet */
28        mping_packet.type = RECEIVER;
29        mping_packet.version_major = htons(VERSION_MAJOR);
30        mping_packet.version_minor = htons(VERSION_MINOR);
31        mping_packet.seq_no = htonl(rcvd_pkt->seq_no);
32        mping_packet.dest_host.s_addr = rcvd_pkt->src_host.s_addr;
33        mping_packet.src_host.s_addr = localIP.s_addr;
34        mping_packet.ttl = rcvd_pkt->ttl;
35        mping_packet.pid = rcvd_pkt->pid;
36        mping_packet.tv.tv_sec = htonl(rcvd_pkt->tv.tv_sec);
37        mping_packet.tv.tv_usec = htonl(rcvd_pkt->tv.tv_usec);
38
39        /* send response packet */
40        send_packet(&mping_packet);
41      }
42    }
43  }
```

mping.c/receiver_listen_loop()

The receiver_listen_loop() function is used to loop indefinitely listening for and responding to mping send packets. Within a loop, a call to recvfrom() is made. When a packet is received, the process_mping_packet() function is called to validate the packet as a valid mping send packet. Once a packet is successfully validated, the reply information is displayed for the user.

The mping response packet is populated using a combination of local data and data from the send packet. The packet type is set to RECEIVER and the version number populated from the header file constants. The destination host address field is populated from the source address field of the send packet, and the source address field is populated with the local address of this recipient. The sequence number, pid, TTL, and timestamp fields are simply echoed back based on what was in the send packet. A call to the send_packet() function sends the packet to the multicast group address.

The next function to look at is clean_exit(). The code is as follows:

mping.c/clean_exit()

```
 1  void clean_exit() {
 2    /* send a DROP MEMBERSHIP message via setsockopt */
 3    if ((setsockopt(sock, IPPROTO_IP, IP_DROP_MEMBERSHIP,
 4        (void*) &mc_request, sizeof(mc_request))) < 0) {
 5      perror("setsockopt() failed");
 6      exit(1);
 7    }
 8
 9    /* close the socket */
10    close(sock);
11
12    /* output statistics and exit program */
13    printf("\n--- mping statistics ---\n");
14    printf("%d packets transmitted, %d packets received\n",
15          packets_sent, packets_rcvd);
16    if (packets_rcvd == 0)
17      printf("round-trip min/avg/max = NA/NA/NA ms\n");
18    else
19      printf("round-trip min/avg/max = %.3f/%.3f/%.3f ms\n",
20            rtt_min, (rtt_total/packets_rcvd), rtt_max);
21    exit(0);
22  }
```

mping.c/clean_exit()

The clean_exit() function cleans up by dropping the group membership, closing the socket, and displaying the run statistics. This function is called when the maximum number of mpings has been sent or the end user generates an interrupt by hitting Control-C.

7.2.1   A Sample Run

All mping requires to run is a flag to indicate if it is in sender or receiver mode. The default TTL is 1. If the program is to be used to perform a test with a large scope, the TTL value needs to be overridden to a higher value using the −t option. A sample run looks like the following:

```
% mping -s -t 5
mping version 1.0
mpinging 239.255.255.1/10000 with ttl=5:

32 bytes from 192.111.52.20: seqno=1 ttl=5 time=1.283 ms
32 bytes from 192.111.52.18: seqno=1 ttl=5 time=1.958 ms
32 bytes from 192.111.52.11: seqno=1 ttl=5 time=2.095 ms
```

```
32 bytes from 192.111.52.15: seqno=1 ttl=5 time=2.224 ms
32 bytes from 192.111.52.20: seqno=2 ttl=5 time=0.567 ms
32 bytes from 192.111.52.18: seqno=2 ttl=5 time=0.901 ms
32 bytes from 192.111.52.15: seqno=2 ttl=5 time=1.046 ms
32 bytes from 192.111.52.11: seqno=2 ttl=5 time=1.176 ms
32 bytes from 192.111.52.20: seqno=3 ttl=5 time=0.709 ms
32 bytes from 192.111.52.18: seqno=3 ttl=5 time=1.060 ms
32 bytes from 192.111.52.15: seqno=3 ttl=5 time=1.196 ms
32 bytes from 192.111.52.11: seqno=3 ttl=5 time=1.328 ms
32 bytes from 192.111.52.20: seqno=4 ttl=5 time=0.629 ms
32 bytes from 192.111.52.18: seqno=4 ttl=5 time=0.976 ms
32 bytes from 192.111.52.11: seqno=4 ttl=5 time=1.111 ms
32 bytes from 192.111.52.15: seqno=4 ttl=5 time=1.241 ms
32 bytes from 192.111.52.20: seqno=5 ttl=5 time=0.463 ms
32 bytes from 192.111.52.18: seqno=5 ttl=5 time=0.828 ms
32 bytes from 192.111.52.15: seqno=5 ttl=5 time=1.033 ms
32 bytes from 192.111.52.11: seqno=5 ttl=5 time=1.178 ms

--- mping statistics ---
5 packets transmitted, 20 packets received
round-trip min/avg/max = 0.463/1.150/2.224 ms
```

In this sample run, the output shows that there were four mping receivers on four different hosts. We transmitted 5 mping packets and received 20 responses. Based on the list of recipients, it appears that there was 0% packet loss among the receivers that responded.[1]

From an individual mping receiver's point of view, the mping run looks like the following:

```
% mping -r
mping version 1.0
Listening on 239.255.255.1/10000:

Replying to mping from 192.111.52.12 bytes=32 seqno=1 ttl=5
Replying to mping from 192.111.52.12 bytes=32 seqno=2 ttl=5
Replying to mping from 192.111.52.12 bytes=32 seqno=3 ttl=5
Replying to mping from 192.111.52.12 bytes=32 seqno=4 ttl=5
Replying to mping from 192.111.52.12 bytes=32 seqno=5 ttl=5
^C
```

7.3 Multicast Scalability

Try the following experiment. Run mping against a single mping receiver on the same LAN, and examine the average time. Then add a handful of mping receivers on the same LAN and repeat

---

[1] This could be validated by storing a hash of each unique IP address and response count, but this is left as an exercise.

the experiment (if necessary, receivers can be added on a single host). Continue adding `mping` receivers and see how the average time is affected.

The likely result was that the average response time began to increase rapidly. Why was this happening? Were the packets actually being returned more slowly? Probably not. A more likely scenario is a combination of contention on the local LAN lines and the ability of the sending `mping` host to deal with many response packets. After all, the `mping` program is not multithreaded, so the packets must be dealt with serially. In other words, the sender is slowly but surely starting to be overwhelmed by responses. In this example, `mping` is sending simple and small response packets. Imagine how much overhead these responses would take if there was more data to be conveyed or the processing of the data was more intensive.

There are a number of approaches to dealing with the kinds of multicast scaling problems just exhibited. The best approach will depend on what the requirements of the particular application are. Here are some general recommendations when designing your multicast application.

- **Understand your limits:** Most important, understand that there are going to be limits on the amount of traffic that hosts and networks can handle. Determine a realistic estimate of what those limits are and how much of those resources an application can reasonably expect to use.

- **Plan for volume:** If an application's traffic requirements are going to be large, do whatever you can to prevent bottlenecks and dropped packets. Increase the system buffer queues, build multithreaded programs to handle packets when appropriate, provision additional bandwidth, and use powerful multiprocessor systems for hardware.

- **Application-level congestion control:** If an application does not require that all feedback be real-time, one useful approach is to stagger responses. Depending on where this is implemented, it is referred to as sender-based or receiver-based congestion control. This topic can be very complex and is discussed next.

7.3.1 Application-Level Congestion Control

With TCP, congestion control is implemented just behind the socket interface; that is, it is implemented between the two hosts without any support from the network. As soon as a TCP socket is opened and data begins being sent, an application programmer knows that data will initially be sent slowly, increase in speed, and back off when packet loss is detected. All this occurs behind the scenes and is essentially transparent to the application. With UDP, there is no congestion control built in because there is no feedback mechanism and so no realization when packets are lost. UDP packets go out as fast as the application and host can send them within the limits of host resources and local network link capacity. Most modern host machines with low-end Ethernet cards are fully capable of sending packets fast enough to saturate a 10-Mbps link.

Since multicast is built on top of UDP, preventing network flooding is entirely up to the design skill and restraint of the application programmer. This means that the sending program should *rate limit* the transmission of packets, in other words, send as much as necessary and reasonable and no more. The general Internet Robustness Principle[2] applies doubly with multicast: "Be liberal in what you accept and conservative in what you send." This also applies to feedback and responses. One approach to building scalable reliability is to use a negative acknowledgment (NAK) scheme as opposed to a positive acknowledgment (ACK) scheme. NAK-based schemes require response packets to be sent when expected data is *not* received, as opposed to acknowledging every single successfully received packet. Another approach used for non-real-time delivery is to use rate-limited sends in multiple phases, allowing each subsequent phase to send only the missed packets [29].

One of the more sophisticated mechanisms of congestion control allows a sender to use feedback from receivers to implement sender-based congestion control. One such algorithm is detailed in RFC 1889, "RTP: A Transport Protocol for Real-Time Applications" [33]. This protocol consists of two components: the Real-Time Transport Protocol (RTP) used to encapsulate real-time data such as streaming video and audio, and the Real-Time Transport Control Protocol (RTCP) for exchanging control information between group members. RTP and RTCP were originally designed with multicast streaming in mind for the experimental multicast backbone. Components of the RTP and RTCP protocols have found their way into most of the commercial streaming applications, including Apple QuickTime, RealNetwork RealSystem, and Microsoft Windows Media. These components are used to provide important functions necessary for supporting multicast-based streaming applications.

The goal of RTP is to encapsulate the streaming data in such a way that reconstruction of the stream (minus packet losses) is possible. This assists in making the stream viewable by receiver(s) and is designed to work over either unicast or multicast. The goal of RTCP is to provide feedback from the recipient(s) of the stream, and to do so in a way that scales from a single unicast receiver to large numbers of multicast receivers. The basic scalability technique is to allow receivers to only periodically transmit reports. The interval between these reports depends on how many other group members are sending reports. These reports include information about the quality of transmission being received, including packet loss and jitter (change in the interval between when packets are received at the destination).

The basis for sender-based congestion control was for these receiver reports to be used at the application layer to scale back the rate at which data is being streamed. However, beyond collecting the feedback, the exact congestion control mechanism is beyond the scope of RTP. But the problem (and solution) of interest is not the congestion control part but the need to prevent the network from being congested with receiver reports when the number of receivers grows arbitrarily large. RTCP provides a mechanism to limit the number of RTCP packets. An algorithm was created by taking into account the number of multicast participants (determined by listening to all the reports sent on the channel), the number of senders, the bandwidth available (assumed to be known by the application), the packet size, and a number of other factors. The result was an interval over which group receivers were told to send their reports. Receivers would multiply this value by a random number between 0.5 and 1.5 to prevent all the receivers from using the same interval. The more members and/or senders, the larger the interval and the less frequently reports would be sent. This prevents control packets

---

[2]Appearing in RFC 1122 [7] and attributed to Internet pioneer Jon Postel.

from overwhelming the session. However, this advantage comes at an obvious cost. The more participants that are in the session, the less frequently reports are received for any individual participant.

The complete algorithm is available in RFC 1889, but in the next section we will implement a simplified version of this algorithm for mping. The goal will be to delay the sending of mping responses based on how much mping traffic we see on the specified mping address. The more mping traffic that is detected, the longer the delay used in sending responses. As with the RTCP algorithm, the delay is adjusted with a random factor to ensure that all replies do not get delayed by the same time period.

7.4   MPing with Receiver-Based Congestion Control

We now show an implementation of mping with receiver-based congestion control. The congestion control we want to implement will introduce a random delay for receivers sending mping responses. The delay should be low when a small number of receivers are detected, and grow with the detection of more receivers. An important consideration is that we do not want any delays due to implosion control to affect the round-trip time calculation.

The first step is to identify the changes to the mping.h header file. In the receiver code, we need to keep track of how long we have delayed the response. Therefore, an additional timeval struct needs to be added to the mping packet definition. This new structure variable is named delay, making the new mping packet structure

```
/* mping packet structure */
struct mping_struct {
  unsigned short version_major;
  unsigned short version_minor;
  unsigned char  type;
  unsigned char  ttl;
  struct in_addr src_host;
  struct in_addr dest_host;
  unsigned int   seq_no;
  pid_t          pid;
  struct timeval tv;
  struct timeval delay;
} mping_packet;
```

Since the packet structure has been changed, the version number is incremented to 1.1. This changes the following constants:

```
#define VERSION_MAJOR 1    /* mping version major */
#define VERSION_MINOR 1    /* mping version minor */
```

Because it is now feasible to delay the response of a sequence of packets such that they are delivered out of order, a single mping packet structure will no longer be a sufficient buffer. Instead, we implement an application-level send buffer. This new structure looks like the following:

```
struct response_buffer {
```

```
    struct mping_struct pkt;
    struct timeval      send_time;
};

#define RESPONSE_BUFFER_SIZE 100

struct response_buffer *resp_buf[RESPONSE_BUFFER_SIZE];
int empty_location=0;
```

The response buffer contains both the mping packets to be sent and a timestamp of when the packet should be sent. The send_time is calculated by adding the current time to the delay time as defined below. We use a default buffer size of 100, and the empty_location variable points to the next available slot in the buffer.

We also need to determine what our bandwidth limit will be for mping. The lower the bandwidth limit, the larger the send delay might be. In order to show some dramatic results with fewer mping recipients, we use 100.0 bytes/second as our bandwidth limit.

```
#define BANDWIDTH 100.0 /* bw in bytes/sec for mping */
```

After making these changes in the header, we are now ready to make changes to the main code. However, before doing this, we need to consider the basic design changes. These include

- Instead of immediately sending response packets, the program should store them in a send buffer along with a time to send. The send time is calculated by adding a computed delay to the current time.

- By using a packet counter and a one-second alarm, the program should determine the number of mping packets that have been received in the last second and then calculate the approximate bandwidth mping is using.

- At the same one-second interval, the program should check the send times of the packets in the send buffer and send any that are ready to go.

Ideally, we would like to check the send times at a more granular level than once per second, but not all systems support more granular timing. In this case, we have continued to use the alarm() function at one-second intervals for portability even though this makes the backoffs somewhat less effective.[3]

The main() function is modified for the receiver code as follows:

```
...
    } else {
        for (x=0; x < RESPONSE_BUFFER_SIZE; x++) resp_buf[x]=NULL;
        signal(SIGALRM, received_packet_count);
        alarm(1);
        receiver_listen_loop();
    }
```

---

[3] In RTCP, the minimum send interval is five seconds, so this is not an issue. Since mping is so basic, we decided intervals of five or more seconds were unnecessary.

First, the send buffer is initialized; then a new function received_packet_count() is set up to catch the alarm signal (remember that previously we only used the alarm signal for the sender, so this does not conflict). The alarm is set to go off in one second, and the code drops into receiver_listen_loop().

The next step is to look at the new version of the receiver_listen_loop() function. The new code is as follows:

mping2.c/receiver_listen_loop()

```
 1  void receiver_listen_loop() {
 2    char recv_packet[MAX_BUF_LEN+1]; /* buffer to receive pkt */
 3    int recv_len;                    /* len of string received */
 4    int x;
 5    double interval;
 6
 7    printf("Listening on %s/%d:\n\n", arg_mcaddr_str, arg_mcport);
 8
 9    while (1) {
10
11      /* clear the receive buffer */
12      memset(recv_packet, 0, sizeof(recv_packet));
13
14      /* block waiting to receive a packet */
15      if ((recv_len = recvfrom(sock, recv_packet, MAX_BUF_LEN,
16          0, NULL, 0)) < 0) {
17        if (errno == EINTR) {
18          /* interrupt is ok */
19          continue;
20        } else {
21          perror("recvfrom() failed");
22          exit(1);
23        }
24      }
25
26      /* process the received packet */
27      if (process_mping_packet(recv_packet, recv_len, SENDER) == 0) {
28        /* packet processed successfully */
29        printf("Received mping from %s bytes=%d seqno=%d ttl=%d\n",
30               inet_ntoa(rcvd_pkt->src_host), recv_len,
31               rcvd_pkt->seq_no, rcvd_pkt->ttl);
32
33        x = empty_location;
34        /* populate mping response packet */
35        if (resp_buf[x] != NULL) {
36          if (verbose) printf("Buffer full, packet dropped\n");
37          continue;
```

```
38            }
39            resp_buf[x] = (struct response_buffer*)
40                        malloc(sizeof(struct response_buffer));
41
42            resp_buf[x]->pkt.type            = RECEIVER;
43            resp_buf[x]->pkt.version_major   = htons(VERSION_MAJOR);
44            resp_buf[x]->pkt.version_minor   = htons(VERSION_MINOR);
45            resp_buf[x]->pkt.seq_no          =
46                             htonl(rcvd_pkt->seq_no);
47            resp_buf[x]->pkt.dest_host.s_addr =
48                                 rcvd_pkt->src_host.s_addr;
49            resp_buf[x]->pkt.src_host.s_addr  = localIP.s_addr;
50            resp_buf[x]->pkt.ttl             = rcvd_pkt->ttl;
51            resp_buf[x]->pkt.pid             = rcvd_pkt->pid;
52            resp_buf[x]->pkt.tv.tv_sec       =
53                                 htonl(rcvd_pkt->tv.tv_sec);
54            resp_buf[x]->pkt.tv.tv_usec      =
55                                 htonl(rcvd_pkt->tv.tv_usec);
56
57            gettimeofday(&resp_buf[x]->send_time, NULL);
58
59            resp_buf[x]->pkt.delay           =
60                                 resp_buf[x]->send_time;
61
62            /* add the random send delay to the send time */
63            interval = send_interval();
64            resp_buf[x]->send_time.tv_sec += (long)interval;
65            resp_buf[x]->send_time.tv_usec +=
66                        (long)((interval-(long)interval)*1000000.0);
67
68            /* increment response buffer pointer */
69            empty_location++;
70            if (empty_location >= RESPONSE_BUFFER_SIZE)
71                empty_location=0;
72        }
73    }
74 }
```

mping2.c/receiver_listen_loop()

The major changes in this function are as follows:

Lines 17–19: Now that we are using the alarm signal for the mping receiver, we need to add code to check for interrupts during the recvfrom() call and continue looping.

Lines 33–40: Preparing the response buffer. We set the variable x to the next position in the send buffer. If the position is already occupied, this means we have wrapped around the entire buffer and it is full.[4] In this case, the packet is simply dropped. If the buffer has space, the memory for the packet is allocated using malloc().

Lines 42–55: Populate the packet in the send buffer in the same manner as the original mping program.

Lines 57–66: Populate the packet's delay field with the current time. This will be used to calculate the total delay later. Compute the send time by adding the current time to the send delay interval returned by send_interval(). The send_interval() function returns a double, which needs to be converted to a timeval structure.

Lines 68–71: Increment the buffer pointer to the next location. If we have exceeded the maximum buffer size, wrap around and start over at zero.

The send_interval() function computes the backoff delay in milliseconds based on the inputs and a random component.

```
double send_interval() {
  double interval;
  const int udp_overhead = 8;
  const int ip_overhead  = 20;
  extern double drand48();

  int packet_size = sizeof(struct mping_struct)
                  + udp_overhead
                  + ip_overhead;

  interval = (packet_size * (double)last_pkt_count / BANDWIDTH);

  return interval * (drand48() + 0.5);
}
```

The delay is determined by multiplying the number of packets seen in the last one-second interval by the packet size divided by the available bandwidth (in bytes/second). The interval is then multiplied by a random number between 0.5 and 1.5 to prevent synchronized backoff. The pseudorandom number generation function recommended by RFC 1889 is drand48(), which is available via stdlib.h.. The packet size is determined by adding the size of the application to the UDP overhead (8 bytes) and IP overhead (20 bytes).

The received_packet_count() function is used to catch the receiver's alarm at one-second intervals. This function looks like the following:

mping2.c/received_packet_count()

```
1  void received_packet_count() {
2    int x;
3
4    /* update the packet count for the last full second */
```

[4] Actually, there may be free slots in the buffer ahead if the later packets are sent first, but we have not implemented a read-ahead buffer check for simplicity.

```
 5    last_pkt_count = curr_pkt_count;
 6
 7    /* reset the current second counter */
 8    curr_pkt_count = 0;
 9
10    /* check if the packets in the send buffer are ready to send */
11    for (x=empty_location; x < RESPONSE_BUFFER_SIZE; x++) {
12      if (resp_buf[x] != NULL) check_send(x);
13    }
14    if (empty_location != 0) {
15      for (x=0; x < empty_location; x++) {
16        if (resp_buf[x] != NULL) check_send(x);
17      }
18    }
19
20    /* reset the alarm */
21    signal(SIGALRM,received_packet_count);
22    alarm(1);
23  }
```

mping2.c/received_packet_count()

Once the alarm is caught, the number of packets seen in the last second is calculated. Then the response buffer is checked for packets ready to send by calling the check_send() function. Finally, the alarm is reset.

The check_send() function is where we check the timestamp on the packets in the buffer to determine if they are ready to send. The code looks like the following:

mping2.c/check_send()

```
 1  void check_send(int x) {
 2    struct timeval now;
 3
 4    gettimeofday(&now, NULL);
 5    if ((resp_buf[x]->send_time.tv_sec < now.tv_sec) ||
 6        ((resp_buf[x]->send_time.tv_sec == now.tv_sec) &&
 7        (resp_buf[x]->send_time.tv_usec <= now.tv_usec))) {
 8
 9      printf("Replying to mping from %s seqno=%d ttl=%d\n",
10            inet_ntoa(resp_buf[x]->pkt.dest_host),
11            ntohl(resp_buf[x]->pkt.seq_no),
12            resp_buf[x]->pkt.ttl);
13
14      subtract_timeval(&now, &resp_buf[x]->pkt.delay);
15      resp_buf[x]->pkt.delay.tv_sec  = htonl(now.tv_sec);
```

```
16    resp_buf[x]->pkt.delay.tv_usec = htonl(now.tv_usec);
17
18    send_packet(&resp_buf[x]->pkt);
19    free(resp_buf[x]);
20    resp_buf[x]=NULL;
21  }
22 }
```

mping2.c/check_send()

The check_send() function gets the current timestamp, then compares that timestamp to the timestamp in the packet it was passed as an argument. If the packet's timestamp is earlier than the current time, it is sent. The reply output message is displayed, and the delay field of the packet is calculated as the delta between the time the packet would have been sent originally and the current time. The send_packet() function is called to send the packet, and then the packet memory is freed and the buffer location emptied.

The final changes needed are to the mping_sender_listen_loop(). The new version of this code is the following:

mping2.c/sender_listen_loop()

```
1  void sender_listen_loop() {
2    char recv_packet[MAX_BUF_LEN+1]; /* buffer to receive packet */
3    int recv_len;                    /* length of packet received */
4    double rtt;                      /* round-trip time */
5    double actual_rtt;               /* rtt - send interval delay */
6
7    while (1) {
8
9      /* clear the receive buffer */
10     memset(recv_packet, 0, sizeof(recv_packet));
11
12     /* block waiting to receive a packet */
13     if ((recv_len = recvfrom(sock, recv_packet, MAX_BUF_LEN,
14         0, NULL, 0)) < 0) {
15       if (errno == EINTR) {
16         /* interrupt is ok */
17         continue;
18       } else {
19         perror("recvfrom() failed");
20         exit(1);
21       }
22     }
23
24     /* get current time */
25     gettimeofday(&current_time, NULL);
```

```
26
27      /* process the received packet */
28      if (process_mping_packet(recv_packet, recv_len, RECEIVER) == 0) {
29
30        /* packet processed successfully */
31
32        /* calculate round-trip time in milliseconds */
33        subtract_timeval(&current_time, &rcvd_pkt->tv);
34        rtt=timeval_to_ms(&current_time);
35
36        /* remove the backoff delay to determine actual rtt */
37        subtract_timeval(&current_time, &rcvd_pkt->delay);
38        actual_rtt = timeval_to_ms(&current_time);
39
40        /* keep rtt total, min and max */
41        rtt_total += actual_rtt;
42        if (actual_rtt > rtt_max) rtt_max = actual_rtt;
43        if (actual_rtt < rtt_min) rtt_min = actual_rtt;
44
45        /* output received packet information */
46        printf("%d bytes from %s: seqno=%d ttl=%d ",
47                recv_len, inet_ntoa(rcvd_pkt->src_host),
48                rcvd_pkt->seq_no, rcvd_pkt->ttl);
49        printf("etime=%.1f ms atime=%.3f ms\n",
50                rtt, actual_rtt);
51      }
52    }
53  }
```

mping2.c/sender_listen_loop()

The sender_listen_loop() function now computes the actual round-trip time (without the backoff-induced delay) in addition to the elapsed time until the packet is received. This is done by first calculating the actual elapsed time and then subtracting the packet's delay timeval structure from the elapsed time. The result is displayed as atime (actual time minus backoff delay) and etime (elapsed time from send to receive).

7.4.1 A Sample Run

The new version of mping is run exactly the same as the old version. Here we show what happens when the sender is run against five receivers.

```
% mping -s -t 5
mping version 1.1
mpinging 239.255.255.1/10000 with ttl=5:
```

```
40 bytes from 192.111.52.20: seqno=1 ttl=5 etime=161.2 ms atime=0.803 ms
40 bytes from 192.111.52.11: seqno=1 ttl=5 etime=382.8 ms atime=1.409 ms
40 bytes from 192.111.52.12: seqno=1 ttl=5 etime=413.8 ms atime=2.518 ms
40 bytes from 192.111.52.15: seqno=1 ttl=5 etime=553.4 ms atime=1.268 ms
40 bytes from 192.111.52.19: seqno=1 ttl=5 etime=608.8 ms atime=1.123 ms
40 bytes from 192.111.52.20: seqno=2 ttl=5 etime=178.4 ms atime=0.569 ms
40 bytes from 192.111.52.11: seqno=2 ttl=5 etime=1389.9 ms atime=0.925 ms
40 bytes from 192.111.52.11: seqno=4 ttl=5 etime=389.8 ms atime=0.856 ms
40 bytes from 192.111.52.12: seqno=2 ttl=5 etime=2421.0 ms atime=1.462 ms
40 bytes from 192.111.52.19: seqno=3 ttl=5 etime=1616.0 ms atime=0.691 ms
40 bytes from 192.111.52.20: seqno=4 ttl=5 etime=1208.2 ms atime=0.547 ms
40 bytes from 192.111.52.12: seqno=3 ttl=5 etime=2422.3 ms atime=2.613 ms
40 bytes from 192.111.52.12: seqno=4 ttl=5 etime=1422.5 ms atime=2.439 ms
40 bytes from 192.111.52.15: seqno=2 ttl=5 etime=3560.7 ms atime=0.969 ms
40 bytes from 192.111.52.15: seqno=3 ttl=5 etime=2561.1 ms atime=1.022 ms
40 bytes from 192.111.52.15: seqno=4 ttl=5 etime=1561.2 ms atime=0.970 ms
40 bytes from 192.111.52.19: seqno=4 ttl=5 etime=1616.4 ms atime=1.097 ms
40 bytes from 192.111.52.20: seqno=3 ttl=5 etime=3218.4 ms atime=0.454 ms
40 bytes from 192.111.52.20: seqno=5 ttl=5 etime=1218.5 ms atime=0.676 ms
40 bytes from 192.111.52.11: seqno=3 ttl=5 etime=3390.0 ms atime=1.076 ms
40 bytes from 192.111.52.11: seqno=5 ttl=5 etime=1390.2 ms atime=1.008 ms
40 bytes from 192.111.52.12: seqno=5 ttl=5 etime=1421.0 ms atime=1.433 ms
40 bytes from 192.111.52.15: seqno=5 ttl=5 etime=1560.6 ms atime=0.885 ms
40 bytes from 192.111.52.19: seqno=2 ttl=5 etime=4616.1 ms atime=0.750 ms
40 bytes from 192.111.52.19: seqno=5 ttl=5 etime=1616.2 ms atime=0.804 ms

--- mping statistics ---
5 packets transmitted, 25 packets received
round-trip min/avg/max = 0.454/1.135/2.613 ms
```

Notice that the response packets' sequence numbers do not fall neatly in order anymore. This indicates our random backoff is working. The elapsed time is recorded, but the actual time measures the round-trip time with the backoff delay excluded.

Here is the run of one of the five receivers.

```
% mping -r -t 5
mping version 1.1
Listening on 239.255.255.1/10000:

Received mping from 192.111.52.12 bytes=40 seqno=1 ttl=5
Replying to mping from 192.111.52.12 seqno=1 ttl=5
Received mping from 192.111.52.12 bytes=40 seqno=2 ttl=5
Received mping from 192.111.52.12 bytes=40 seqno=3 ttl=5
Received mping from 192.111.52.12 bytes=40 seqno=4 ttl=5
Received mping from 192.111.52.12 bytes=40 seqno=5 ttl=5
Replying to mping from 192.111.52.12 seqno=2 ttl=5
Replying to mping from 192.111.52.12 seqno=3 ttl=5
Replying to mping from 192.111.52.12 seqno=5 ttl=5
Replying to mping from 192.111.52.12 seqno=4 ttl=5
```

7.4.2 Design Notes

There are several things to consider about the design of this type of congestion control. One is that the application must be able to withstand the increased delay in receiving packets as the number of recipients increases. With mping this was simple to overcome by separating the actual and elapsed round-trip times. There may be a certain threshold where an application cannot operate effectively with the introduced latency. At this point, the design must be reevaluated or the send interval algorithm made more aggressive at the risk of consuming more resources.

A second consideration is the fact that not all hosts may have all the information required to scale back properly. Consider a simple inter-domain example where a host is attached to two routers with recipients on the other side of each router. If the sender is transmitting with a TTL of 2, it can reach the recipients on either side of each router, but the recipients on each side cannot reach each other (see Figure 7.1). In wireless communication, this is commonly called the hidden station problem.

This will give the recipients on both sides an incorrect view of the number of participants in the multicast session. As a result, if the application requires accurate group size estimation

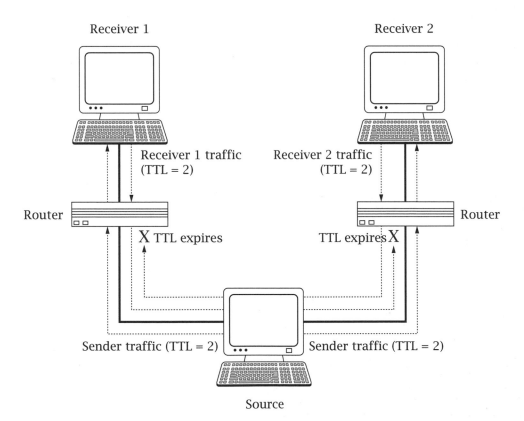

Figure 7.1 TTL scoping with a network topology that hides some participants from each other.

for congestion control, it should ensure that the TTL is large enough not only for the sources to reach all receivers, but also for all receivers to reach all other receivers.

7.5 Exercises

1. By running `mping` in verbose mode (–v), you can see that `mping` handles discarding its own packets at the application level. How could this be handled at the IP level instead? Modify the program to do this. How does this change impact the feedback mechanism?

2. Write an `mping` program in Java or C#.

3. One mechanism to determine the exact TTL between two hosts is to test connectivity with increasing TTLs (starting at 1 and increasing until connectivity is established). Modify the `mping` program to perform this type of test. Explain why the exact TTL required between two hosts might change dynamically.

4. If you are using a system that supports timers at a finer granularity than one second, modify `mping` to perform backoffs at a finer time granularity. How does this impact performance?

5. The hidden station problem also has implications for session announcements and the selection of pseudorandom group addresses. Describe a scenario in which address collision occurs even though a host is listening to other advertised sessions.

6. What are some mechanisms to determine the absence of a multicast `ping` reply? (Hint: group membership must be known.)

7. Modify the `mping` program to report detailed loss statistics by receiver.

chapter 8

Application-Layer Multicast and Reflectors

At this point, we have covered almost everything a programmer needs to know in order to write a reasonably robust multicast application. This includes how to open the sockets, how to scope packet transmissions, what multicast group to use, new interfaces for Source Specific Multicast, and the beginnings of how to deal with many-to-one feedback. One key assumption is that all routers are multicast capable. The obvious problem is that this is not an accurate assumption for the current Internet. Therefore, we now turn our attention to enabling one-to-many communication between a source and a group of hosts, of which only some have multicast connectivity.

The last code example presented in this book merges the topics of reflectors and application-layer multicast. Reflectors are designed to receive one transmission and "reflect" it multiple times. Application-layer multicast is one-to-many communication supported by application-layer mechanisms. Multicast that uses router support for building and maintaining trees is typically called native multicast or network-layer multicast.

8.1 Introduction

The idea of application-layer multicast has again become popular. Why "again"? Because the original multicast backbone (MBone) was an application-layer overlay at its inception (see Appendix A for a full history). The MBone consisted of a set of hosts that were responsible for creating multicast trees and performing packet replication. The concept has been repeated numerous times in other applications (USENET news, email exploders, etc.).

The MBone was augmented and eventually replaced by network-layer multicast. As routers were enhanced to provide multicast support, small islands of multicast-capable routers grew into continents. The goal is (still) to one day have no islands.

Using network-layer multicast has several advantages over application-layer multicast. First, the branching points are not limited to the edges of the network. If only hosts are able to provide this functionality, the trees that are built become significantly different from reverse shortest path trees. Second, hosts do not route, forward, or replicate packets as efficiently as routers. Passing packets to the application layer significantly increases overhead, complexity, jitter, delay, and loss. Why then is application-layer multicast making a comeback?

Application-layer multicast is again becoming popular because the deployment of network-layer multicast has been far slower than expected. There are a number of reasons, and the study of these reasons has even been the subject of a magazine article [15]. The bottom line is that there are several "chicken-and-egg" problems that prevent Internet Service Providers (ISPs) from wanting to deploy a service that only a few applications can utilize. And as for the application developers, no one wants to build applications that use a service that is not widely available to users. A good analogy here is the deployment of IPv6 versus Network Address Translators (NATs). IPv6 is the right solution technically speaking, but it is very hard to deploy. NAT is a bad solution for a number of reasons, but it is easy for users to deploy, and it solves the primary problem of IP address scarcity.

From a multicast perspective, reflectors may be a bad idea. The better solution would be to deploy multicast end to end. However, only an idealist would be able to ignore the futility of achieving end-to-end multicast deployment everywhere. Therefore, in this chapter, we present a simple reflector, in essence an application-layer multicast device.

A multicast reflector requires two functions. The first function is to determine the set of receiving IP addresses that want multicast traffic from a particular group (and possibly a specific source, too). The second function is to join the multicast group and then create an individualized stream for each receiver. Obviously, the reflector needs to be run on a machine that has multicast connectivity and enough bandwidth to create a replicated stream for each receiver.

There are two scenarios in which to run a reflector. In one case, multicast is available to the reflector but not between the reflector and the set of receivers. This is the obvious case when someone thinks of a reflector. The second case is when there is only unicast to the reflector but multicast capability between the reflector and the set of receivers. The first case is a true reflector. The second case is more of a gateway and is used to avoid numerous redundant streams coming over an external link—a link over which bandwidth is likely expensive and scarce.

8.2 A Multicast Reflector in Java

We now introduce a multicast reflector in Java that can operate in either mode listed earlier. In MULTI_TO_UNI (MULTIcast-TO-UNIcast) mode, packets on a specified multicast address are unicast to a list of receivers. In UNI_TO_MULTI (UNIcast-TO-MULTIcast) mode, packets received via a unicast transmission are forwarded on a multicast address. These modes could be used in a stand-alone manner, especially to extend the reachability of a multicast stream to connect a small number of receivers that do not have multicast. Receivers could subscribe to a multicast address, and if it is not within a multicast-connected area of the network, its address can be

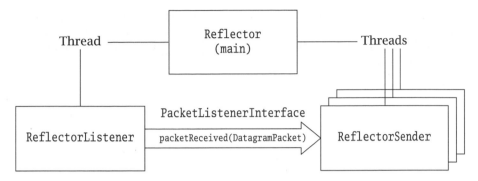

Figure 8.1 Basic architecture of the reflector program.

added to the reflector as a unicast feed.[1] There are limits to how scalable this approach can be since the more receivers that are located outside the multicast-enabled network the quicker the scenario degrades to unicast only (and all the inherent scalability issues).

A more useful approach is to use the two modes in conjunction. Two multicast-capable subnets each run an instance of the reflector. One runs in MULTI_TO_UNI mode, and the other runs in UNI_TO_MULTI mode. The two reflector instances essentially build a tunnel between themselves. This can be remarkably useful when many of a group's receivers are located on a small number of subnets. If this is the case, bandwidth can still be saved by sending packets once to each of the subnets and then multicasting them to all recipients on the local subnet. As an aside, most commercial streaming servers can support some manner of multicast tunneling today.

The reflector functionality we just discussed is also similar to a program called *mrouted*. *Mrouted* is the multicast routing demon. It was used to create multicast tunnels in the original MBone. *Mrouted* was in fact very sophisticated in that it was acting as an actual router and was capable of responding to IGMP packets and running a routing protocol.

Our reflector example is fairly straightforward and determines routes statically using a configuration file. The basic architecture is shown in Figure 8.1.

Reflector.java contains the main function and the core logic. It reads and validates the configuration file and spawns the appropriate threads to listen for and forward packets. One thread is spawned for each send address. When packets are received, they are passed to the forwarding threads by using an interface class PacketReceiverInterface. This interface defines a single method, packetReceived(), which takes a DatagramPacket as an argument. Some additional utility classes include Address.java for storing an IP address/port pair and Logger.java for logging packets.

---

[1] There have been a number of subscription mechanisms proposed over the years, but by far the most ubiquitous is now the Web.

Note that for simplicity we have opted to send the unicast packets over UDP, but since this is a unicast point-to-point connection, this is not required. Depending on the requirements of the particular application, it may be beneficial to use TCP on the point-to-point links to take advantage of TCP's reliability features.

We'll start by looking at the utility class Address.java.

Address.java

```
1   import java.net.*;
2
3   // Address class is used to store an IP address and port
4   // combination.
5
6   public class Address {
7
8     private InetAddress address = null;
9     private int         port    = 0;
10
11    public Address(InetAddress address, int port) {
12      this.address = address;
13      this.port    = port;
14    }
15
16    public Address(InetAddress address) {
17      this.address = address;
18    }
19
20    public Address(int port) {
21      this.port    = port;
22    }
23
24    public InetAddress getAddress() { return(address); }
25    public int         getPort() { return(port); }
26
27    public void setPort(int port) {
28      this.port    = port;
29    }
30
31    public void setAddress(InetAddress address) {
32      this.address = address;
33    }
34
35    public boolean isComplete() {
36      // return true if both IP and port are populated,
37      // false otherwise.
38
```

```
39    if ((address != null) && (port != 0))
40       return(true);
41    else
42       return(false);
43  }
44
45  public String toString() {
46    // return a string representation of the IP/port.
47
48    String str;
49
50    if (address == null)
51      str = "";
52    else
53      str = address.getHostAddress();
54
55    str = str + "/" + port;
56
57    return(str);
58  }
59 }
```

Address.java

The Address class is used to store an IP address and port combination.[2] Its constructor is overloaded to take both or either argument. There are get and set methods (getAddress(), setAddress(), getPort(), and setPort()) for retrieving and setting the values in an already instantiated class. The isComplete() method returns true if both the address and port have been populated, and false otherwise. The toString() method returns a string representation of the combination.

Next we look at Reflector.java, which contains the main logic of the reflector program.

Reflector.java

```
1  import java.io.*;
2  import java.net.*;
3  import java.util.*;
4
5  public class Reflector implements Runnable {
6
7    // valid names found in the config file:
```

---

[2] In Java 2 v1.4, the SocketAddress class can be used to similar effect.

```
 8     public static final String MODE        = "Mode";
 9     public static final String SOURCE_IP   = "SourceIP";
10     public static final String SOURCE_PORT = "SourcePort";
11     public static final String DEST_IP     = "DestIP";
12     public static final String DEST_PORT   = "DestPort";
13
14     // valid modes in the config file, unicast to
15     // multicast or multicast to unicast
16     public static final String INPUT_UNITOMULTI = "UNI_TO_MULTI";
17     public static final String INPUT_MULTITOUNI = "MULTI_TO_UNI";
18
19     // possible modes the reflector can be set to:
20     public static final int MODE_NONE        = 0;
21     public static final int MODE_UNI_TO_MULTI = 1;
22     public static final int MODE_MULTI_TO_UNI = 2;
23
24     // variables to indicate source or destination
25     public static final int SOURCE = 1;
26     public static final int DEST   = 2;
27
28     // min and max network ports allowed
29     public static final int MIN_PORT =  1024;
30     public static final int MAX_PORT = 65095;
31
32     // which mode the reflector is being run in:
33     private int mode=0;
34
35     // source and destination hold variables:
36     private Address source;
37     private Hashtable dest;
38     private Address hold_dest=null;
39
40     // logging toggle and logger class
41     boolean logging=true;
42     Logger logger;
43
44     public Reflector() {}
45
46     public void run() {
47       // validate the config file
48       if (readConfig() != 0) {
49         System.err.println("Error parsing config file\n");
50         System.exit(-1);
51       }
52
53       // start the logger
54       logger = new Logger(logging);
```

```
55
56      // spawn a thread to listen for packets
57      ReflectorListener listener = new ReflectorListener(source,
58                                                         mode,
59                                                         logger);
60      System.out.println("Listening on " + source.toString());
61
62      // spawn threads for each source address packets
63      // are to be forwarded on. Register each thread as
64      // PacketListenerInterface with the listener thread.
65      System.out.println("Sending on:");
66      for (Enumeration e = dest.elements(); e.hasMoreElements();) {
67        Address a = (Address)e.nextElement();
68        ReflectorSender sender = new ReflectorSender(a, mode,
69                                                     logger);
70        sender.start();
71        listener.addPacketListener((PacketListenerInterface)sender);
72        System.out.println("          " + a.toString());
73      }
74
75      // start the listener
76      listener.start();
77    }
78
79    public int readConfig() {
80      // validate the contents of the config file
81
82      BufferedReader input=null;
83      String name, value, inputLine=null;
84
85      dest=new Hashtable();
86
87      // open and read the config file
88      try {
89        input = new BufferedReader(new FileReader("reflector.conf"));
90        inputLine=input.readLine();
91      } catch (IOException e) {
92        System.err.println("Error reading reflector.conf.");
93        return(-1);
94      }
95
96      // loop until entire config file is read
97      while (inputLine != null) {
98
99        // skip comments:
100       if (inputLine.charAt(0) != '#') {
101
```

```
102        // extract a name/value pair, and branch
103        // based on the name:
104
105        StringTokenizer tokenizer =
106                        new StringTokenizer(inputLine,"=");
107        name = tokenizer.nextToken();
108        value = tokenizer.nextToken();
109
110        if (name == null) {
111          System.out.println("no name");
112          continue;
113        } else if (name.equals(MODE)) {
114          if (setMode(value) != 0) {
115            System.err.println("Error setting mode to " + value);
116            return(-1);
117          }
118        } else if (name.equals(SOURCE_IP)) {
119          if (setSourceIP(value) != 0) {
120            System.err.println("Error setting src IP address to "
121                          + value);
122            return(-1);
123          }
124        } else if (name.equals(SOURCE_PORT)) {
125          if (setSourcePort(value) != 0) {
126            System.err.println("Error setting src port to "
127                          + value);
128            return(-1);
129          }
130        } else if (name.equals(DEST_IP)) {
131          if (setDestIP(value) != 0) {
132            System.err.println("Error setting dest IP address to "
133                          + value);
134            return(-1);
135          }
136        } else if (name.equals(DEST_PORT)) {
137          if (setDestPort(value) != 0) {
138            System.err.println("Error setting dest port to "
139                          + value);
140            return(-1);
141          }
142        } else {
143          System.err.println("Skipping invalid config file value: "
144                          + name);
145        }
146      }
147      // read next line in the config file
148      try {
```

```
149        inputLine=input.readLine();
150      } catch (IOException e) {
151        System.err.println("Error reading reflector.conf.");
152        return(-1);
153      }
154    }
155
156    // close the config file
157    try {
158      input.close();
159    } catch (IOException e) {
160      System.err.println("Error closing reflector.conf.");
161      return(-1);
162    }
163
164    // validate that the combined contents of the config file
165    // make sense
166    if (! isConfigValid()) {
167      System.err.println("Configuration file is not complete.");
168      return(-1);
169    }
170    return(0);
171  }
172
173  private int setMode(String value) {
174    // validate and set the mode from the config file
175    if (value.equals(INPUT_UNITOMULTI)) {
176      mode = MODE_UNI_TO_MULTI;
177      return(0);
178    } else if (value.equals(INPUT_MULTITOUNI)) {
179      mode = MODE_MULTI_TO_UNI;
180      return(0);
181    } else {
182      return(-1);
183    }
184  }
185
186  private int setSourceIP(String value) {
187    // validate and set the source IP from the config file
188
189    // call modeToAddress to validate IP address
190    InetAddress inet = modeToAddress(value,SOURCE);
191    if (inet == null) return(-1);
192
193    if (source != null) {
194      if (source.getAddress() != null)
195        System.err.println("Warning: overwriting src address " +
```

```
196                              source.getAddress().getHostAddress()
197                              + " with " +
198                              inet.getHostAddress() + ".");
199          source.setAddress(inet);
200        } else {
201          source = new Address(inet);
202        }
203
204        return(0);
205      }
206
207      private int setSourcePort(String value) {
208        // validate and set the source port from the config file
209
210        int port;
211
212        try {
213          port = Integer.parseInt(value);
214        } catch (NumberFormatException nfe) {
215          return(-1);
216        }
217
218        if ((port < MIN_PORT) || (port > 65095))
219          return(-1);
220
221        if (source != null) {
222          if (source.getPort() != 0)
223            System.err.println("Warning: overwriting src port " +
224                               source.getPort() + " with port " +
225                               port + ".");
226          source.setPort(port);
227        } else {
228          source = new Address(port);
229        }
230
231        return(0);
232      }
233
234      private int setDestIP(String value) {
235        // validate and set the dest IP from the config file
236
237        // call modeToAddress to validate IP address
238        InetAddress inet = modeToAddress(value,DEST);
239        if (inet == null) return(-1);
240
241        if (hold_dest != null) {
242          if (hold_dest.getAddress() != null)
```

```
243            System.err.println("Warning: overwriting dest address " +
244                             hold_dest.getAddress().getHostAddress()
245                             + " with " +
246                             inet.getHostAddress() + ".");
247        hold_dest.setAddress(inet);
248        if (hold_dest.isComplete())
249          return(addDest());
250     } else {
251        hold_dest = new Address(inet);
252     }
253     return(0);
254   }
255
256   private int setDestPort(String value) {
257     // validate and set the dest port from the config file
258
259     int port;
260
261     try {
262       port = Integer.parseInt(value);
263     } catch (NumberFormatException nfe) {
264       return(-1);
265     }
266
267     if ((port < MIN_PORT) || (port > MAX_PORT))
268       return(-1);
269
270     if (hold_dest != null) {
271        if (hold_dest.getPort() != 0)
272          System.err.println("Warning: overwriting dest port " +
273                             hold_dest.getPort() + " with port "
274                             + port + ".");
275        hold_dest.setPort(port);
276        if (hold_dest.isComplete())
277          return(addDest());
278     } else {
279        hold_dest = new Address(port);
280     }
281
282     return(0);
283   }
284
285   private int addDest() {
286     // once both a dest IP and port have been read, add them
287     // to our vector of all destinations.
288
289     switch(mode) {
```

```
290        case MODE_UNI_TO_MULTI:
291          if (!dest.isEmpty()) {
292            System.err.println("Warning: dest address overwritten");
293            dest.clear();
294          }
295          dest.put(hold_dest.toString(),hold_dest);
296          break;
297        case MODE_MULTI_TO_UNI:
298          dest.put(hold_dest.toString(),hold_dest);
299          break;
300        default:
301          // no mode set
302          System.err.println("Destination " +
303                             hold_dest.toString() +
304                             " skipped because no mode set.");
305          hold_dest=null;
306          return(-1);
307      }
308      hold_dest=null;
309      return(0);
310    }
311
312    private InetAddress modeToAddress(String value, int type) {
313      // validate the IP address based on its text value, its
314      // type (DEST or SOURCE), and the mode (UNI_TO_MULTI or
315      // MULTI_TO_UNI). Returns an InetAddress if successful and
316      // null on failure.
317
318      InetAddress inet;
319
320      if ((type != DEST) && (type != SOURCE)) {
321        System.err.println("Invalid type passed to modeToAddress ("
322                           + type + ")");
323        return(null);
324      }
325
326      switch(mode) {
327        case MODE_UNI_TO_MULTI:
328          if (type == DEST)
329            inet = returnValidMCIP(value);
330          else
331            inet = returnValidIP(value);
332          break;
333        case MODE_MULTI_TO_UNI:
334          if (type == DEST)
335            inet = returnValidIP(value);
336          else
```

```
337           inet = returnValidMCIP(value);
338         break;
339       default:
340         // no mode set
341         System.err.println("Error: No Mode Selected.");
342         return(null);
343     }
344
345     if (inet == null)
346       System.err.println("Invalid dest IP address (" +
347                          value + ").");
348
349     return(inet);
350   }
351
352   private InetAddress returnValidIP(String IP) {
353     // return InetAddress if IP is valid, null otherwise
354
355     InetAddress inet;
356     try {
357       inet = InetAddress.getByName(IP);
358     } catch (UnknownHostException e) {
359       return(null);
360     }
361     return(inet);
362   }
363
364   private InetAddress returnValidMCIP(String IP) {
365     // return InetAddress if IP is valid multicast addr,
366     // null otherwise
367
368     InetAddress inet = returnValidIP(IP);
369     if (inet.isMulticastAddress()) {
370       return(inet);
371     } else {
372       return(null);
373     }
374   }
375
376   public boolean isConfigValid() {
377     // validate that the mode, source IP/port, and
378     // dest IP(s)/port(s) are all valid and a valid
379     // combination.
380
381     if (mode == MODE_NONE) {
382       System.err.println("No mode selected.");
383       return(false);
```

```
384      }
385      if (! source.isComplete()) {
386        if ((source.getPort() != 0) &&
387            (mode == MODE_UNI_TO_MULTI)) {
388          // if source is unicast local IP is implied
389          try {
390            source.setAddress(InetAddress.getLocalHost());
391          } catch (UnknownHostException e) {
392            System.err.println("Incomplete source address.");
393            return(false);
394          }
395        } else {
396          System.err.println("Incomplete source address.");
397          return(false);
398        }
399      }
400      if (dest.isEmpty()) {
401        System.err.println("No destination addresses.");
402        return(false);
403      }
404      for (Enumeration e = dest.elements(); e.hasMoreElements();) {
405        Address a = (Address)e.nextElement();
406        if (! a.isComplete()) {
407          System.err.println("Incomplete destination address.");
408          return(false);
409        }
410      }
411      return(true);
412    }
413
414    public static void main(String args[]) {
415      Reflector r = new Reflector();
416      r.run();
417    }
418  }
```

Reflector.java

The main() function and most of the main logic reside in the Reflector class. The main() function simply creates an instance of a Reflector class and starts it with the run() method. The Reflector constructor takes no arguments and calls the readConfig() method to read and validate the Reflector configuration file (reflector.conf, which needs to reside in the run directory). The configuration file and its syntax are described in more detail later.

Once the configuration file is validated, a Logger class is created to handle opening and writing to a log file (reflector.log). A boolean called logging is used to toggle logging on and off.

The last function of the `Reflector` constructor code is to set up a thread to listen for packets, as many threads as are necessary to forward packets and to establish communication between them. Regardless of whether the incoming packets are on a unicast address or a multicast address, the `Reflector` allows only one input source. In lines 56-60, a single `ReflectorListener` thread is started. The arguments are the source, the mode (`UNI_TO_MULTI` or `MULTI_TO_UNI`), and the logger class instance to log activity.

In lines 62-73, the list of all the destination addresses is parsed and a new `ReflectorSender` thread started for each address. In addition to creating these threads, each thread is registered through a `PacketListenerInterface` by passing it to the `ReflectorListener` method `addPacketListener()`. This interface is discussed in more detail later, but it essentially allows sending threads to be notified every time a new packet to be reflected has arrived.

The configuration parsing takes up the bulk of the code in `Reflector.java` but is fairly straightforward. The `readConfig()` method opens reflector.conf and parses it line by line. A 0 is returned if it is successfully parsed, a −1 on failure. Each line of the configuration file is a simple list of name/value pairs separated by an equal sign (=). The name/value pairs are case sensitive, and no extraneous white space (other than newlines) should occur in the file. A pound sign (#) as the first byte of a line is a comment and is ignored. The valid name/value pairs are

- Mode: Set to either `MULTI_TO_UNI` (multicast input reflected to one or more unicast outputs) or `UNI_TO_MULTI` (unicast input reflected to a multicast channel).

- SourceIP: An IP address of the reflector source. This should be a multicast address in `MULTI_TO_UNI` mode and a unicast IP address in `UNI_TO_MULTI` mode. If the `SourceIP` field is omitted in `UNI_TO_MULTI` mode, the local IP address will be used as the source. This supports the case where the reflector is being run on the same machine as is sourcing the packets.

- SourcePort: The port of the reflector source.

- DestIP: One or more destination IP addresses to reflect packets to. In `UNI_TO_MULTI` mode, this must be a multicast IP address. In `MULTI_TO_UNI` mode, this must be a unicast IP address. `DestIP` and `DestPort` fields should always appear in consecutive pairs.

- DestPort: One or more destination ports on which to reflect packets. `DestIP` and `DestPort` fields should always appear in consecutive pairs.

A sample `reflector.conf` file is

```
# My Sample reflector.conf file
Mode=MULTI_TO_UNI
SourceIP=239.255.10.10
SourcePort=10000
DestIP=192.111.43.37
DestPort=10001
DestIP=192.111.43.38
DestPort=10002
```

In this example, we are taking packets on multicast address 239.255.10.10:10000 and forwarding them using unicast to two hosts at 192.111.43.37:10001 and 192.111.43.38:10002.

Depending on what name we have parsed, one of a number of methods to validate and store the configuration values is called: setMode(), setSourceIP(), setSourcePort(), setDestIP(), or setDestPort(). Two utility methods, returnValidIP() and returnValidMCIP(), are used to create and validate unicast or multicast IP addresses, respectively. The isConfigValid() method is called when the configuration file has been parsed to ensure that the combined configuration options are valid. It returns true if they are valid, and false if they are not.

The next class is PacketListenerInterface.java. The code is as follows:

PacketListenerInterface.java

```
1  import java.net.DatagramPacket;
2
3  // PacketListenerInterface used by threads that need to
4  // be notified of datagram packet receipt. A single
5  // interface function packetReceived passes the packet
6  // information to the thread requiring the information.
7
8  public interface PacketListenerInterface {
9    public void packetReceived(DatagramPacket packet);
10 }
```

PacketListenerInterface.java

The PacketListenerInterface is a simple interface used to pass information from the ReflectorListener thread to the ReflectorSender threads. It contains a single method called packetReceived(), which takes a DatagramPacket argument. The ReflectorSender class implements this interface by defining a packetReceived() method, and the ReflectorSender class uses the interface by keeping a list of all registered interfaces and calling the method when a packet is received.

The next class is ReflectorListener.java. The code is as follows:

ReflectorListener.java

```
1  import java.io.*;
2  import java.net.*;
3  import java.util.*;
4
5  // ReflectorListener thread listens for packets
6  // and notifies one or more interested threads
7  // who register as PacketListenerInterfaces.
8
9  public class ReflectorListener extends Thread {
10   private InetAddress listenAddr;
```

```
11    private int        listenPort;
12    private int        mode;
13
14    private Vector      packetListeners;
15    private Logger      logger;
16
17    private static final int MAX_PACKET_SIZE = 1500;
18
19    public ReflectorListener(Address a, int mode, Logger logger) {
20      listenAddr  = a.getAddress();
21      listenPort  = a.getPort();
22      this.mode   = mode;
23      this.logger = logger;
24
25      packetListeners = new Vector();
26    }
27
28    public void run() {
29      // create a unicast or multicast socket
30      // depending on the mode and listen for packets.
31
32      switch (mode) {
33      case Reflector.MODE_UNI_TO_MULTI:
34        DatagramSocket ds = initUnicastSocket();
35        if (ds != null) listen(ds);
36        break;
37      case Reflector.MODE_MULTI_TO_UNI:
38        MulticastSocket mc = initMulticastSocket();
39        if (mc != null) listen((DatagramSocket)mc);
40        break;
41      default:
42        break;
43      }
44    }
45
46    private MulticastSocket initMulticastSocket() {
47      // initialize a MulticastSocket and join the group
48
49      MulticastSocket mc;
50      try {
51        mc = new MulticastSocket(listenPort);
52        mc.joinGroup(listenAddr);
53      } catch (Exception e) {
54        System.err.println("Failed to create MulticastSocket on " +
55                           "port " + listenPort);
56        return(null);
57      }
58      return(mc);
59    }
```

```
60
61    private DatagramSocket initUnicastSocket() {
62      // initialize a DatagramSocket
63
64      DatagramSocket ds;
65      try {
66        ds = new DatagramSocket(listenPort);
67      } catch (Exception e) {
68        System.err.println("Failed to create DatagramSocket on "
69                           + "port " + listenPort);
70        return(null);
71      }
72      return(ds);
73    }
74
75    private void listen(DatagramSocket ds) {
76      // loop forever listening to packets, when they
77      // arrive log them and notify all interested threads.
78
79      byte[] buffer;
80      DatagramPacket packet;
81
82      while (true) {
83        try {
84          buffer = new byte[MAX_PACKET_SIZE];
85          packet = new DatagramPacket(buffer, buffer.length);
86
87          ds.receive(packet);
88
89          logger.log("Packet received, " + packet.getLength()
90                     + " bytes");
91          eventNotify(packet);
92
93        } catch (IOException e) {
94          System.err.println("Error receiving packet\n");
95          e.printStackTrace();
96        }
97      }
98    }
99
100   public void addPacketListener(PacketListenerInterface pl) {
101     // add interested thread to listeners vector
102     packetListeners.addElement(pl);
103   }
104
105   public void removePacketListener(PacketListenerInterface pl) {
106     // remove thread to listeners vector
107     packetListeners.removeElement(pl);
108   }
```

```
109
110    private void eventNotify(DatagramPacket packet) {
111      // notify all registered threads that a packet has arrived
112      // using the packetReceived(DatagramPacket) method.
113
114      for (Enumeration e = packetListeners.elements();
115           e.hasMoreElements(); ) {
116
117        PacketListenerInterface pl =
118                    (PacketListenerInterface) e.nextElement();
119        pl.packetReceived(packet);
120      }
121    }
122  }
```

ReflectorListener.java

The ReflectorListener class runs as its own thread. When the thread is started with the run() method, either a unicast DatagramSocket or a MulticastSocket is created based on the mode. We have not discussed the DatagramSocket class, but it is a superclass of the Multicast-Socket class, and they share most of the core methods. An initUnicastSocket() method or initMulticastSocket() method is used to create the appropriate socket. The only functional difference between the two, other than the socket class used, is that the MulticastSocket adds a call to the joinGroup() method. If the socket creation step is successful, the listen() method is invoked with the socket as an argument. Since the MulticastSocket is extended from the DatagramSocket, we can set the argument type to DatagramSocket and cast the MulticastSocket to its parent class.

The listen() method loops listening for packets using the receive() method. When a packet is received, it is logged and the eventNotify() method is called with the packet as an argument.

The eventNotify() method is used to invoke the PacketListenerInterface and notify all registered ReflectorSender threads that a packet has arrived. The list of all registered ReflectorSender threads is stored in the packetListeners vector. The eventNotify() method first checks the vector size to ensure that there are threads to notify. Then each listener is passed a reference to the received packet using the packetReceived() method.

The addPacketListener() and removePacketListener() methods allow the ReflectorSender threads to add themselves to and remove themselves from the list of registered packet listeners.

The next class is ReflectorSender.java. The code is as follows:

ReflectorSender.java

```
1  import java.net.*;
2  import java.io.*;
3
4  // ReflectorSender creates a unicast or multicast socket
```

```
 5   // and is registered to receive incoming packet notifications
 6   // via the PacketListenerInterface. Incoming packets
 7   // are forwarded on the outgoing socket.
 8
 9   public class ReflectorSender extends Thread
10                              implements PacketListenerInterface {
11     private InetAddress sendAddr;
12     private int         sendPort;
13     private int         mode;
14
15     private DatagramSocket ds=null;
16     private Logger logger;
17
18     public ReflectorSender(Address a, int mode, Logger logger) {
19       sendAddr    = a.getAddress();
20       sendPort    = a.getPort();
21       this.mode   = mode;
22       this.logger = logger;
23     }
24
25     public void run() {
26       // initialize a DatagramSocket or MulticastSocket
27       // based on the mode:
28
29       switch (mode) {
30       case Reflector.MODE_MULTI_TO_UNI:
31         ds = initUnicastSocket();
32         break;
33       case Reflector.MODE_UNI_TO_MULTI:
34         ds = (DatagramSocket) initMulticastSocket();
35         break;
36       default:
37         break;
38       }
39     }
40
41     private MulticastSocket initMulticastSocket() {
42       // initialize a MulticastSocket
43
44       MulticastSocket mc;
45       try {
46         mc = new MulticastSocket(sendPort);
47       } catch (Exception e) {
48         e.printStackTrace();
49         return(null);
50       }
51       return(mc);
52     }
53
```

```
54    private DatagramSocket initUnicastSocket() {
55      // initialize a DatagramSocket
56
57      DatagramSocket ds;
58      try {
59        ds = new DatagramSocket(sendPort);
60      } catch (Exception e) {
61        e.printStackTrace();
62        return(null);
63      }
64      return(ds);
65    }
66
67    public void packetReceived(DatagramPacket packet) {
68      // An incoming packet has been received. Override
69      // the old packet addressing to the new outgoing
70      // addressing, send it and log it.
71
72      try {
73        packet.setAddress(sendAddr);
74        packet.setPort(sendPort);
75        ds.send(packet);
76        logger.log("Packet forwarded to " +
77                  packet.getAddress().getHostAddress() + "/" +
78                  packet.getPort() + ", " + packet.getLength()
79                  + " bytes");
80      } catch (IOException e) {
81        System.err.println("Error sending packet");
82        e.printStackTrace();
83      }
84    }
85  }
```

ReflectorSender.java

One ReflectorSender instance is created for each unique outbound reflector address and runs as its own thread. When the thread is started with the run() method, either a unicast DatagramSocket or a MulticastSocket is created based on the mode. An initUnicastSocket() method or initMulticastSocket() method is used to create the appropriate socket.

After the socket is created, the thread simply waits to be informed of packets to forward by the PacketListenerInterface. Each ReflectorSender thread is registered as a PacketListenerInterface to the ReflectorListener thread by the main program logic. When the receivedPacket() method of the ReflectorSender is invoked, the packet is passed as the argument. Remember, in Java the DatagramPacket class contains the addressing information in it, so before sending it the packet's old addressing information should be overwritten with the new destination IP address and port number using the setAddress() and setPort() methods of

DatagramPacket. Next, the send() method is invoked to send the packet on its way. And, finally, the packet is logged if the logging option is set.

The final class is Logger.java. The code is as follows:

Logger.java

```
1   import java.io.*;
2   import java.util.*;
3
4   // Logger class opens and writes to the log file
5   // if boolean true is passed as constructor argument.
6
7   public class Logger {
8
9     private boolean    logging;
10    private FileWriter logfile;
11
12    public Logger(boolean logging) {
13      this.logging = logging;
14
15      if (logging) {
16        try {
17          // open logfile for append
18          logfile=new FileWriter("reflector.log", true);
19        } catch (IOException e) {
20          System.err.println("Error opening log file.");
21        }
22        log("Reflector started: " + new Date());
23      }
24    }
25
26    public void log(String str) {
27      // write string to log file
28
29      // if logging disabled return
30      if (!logging) return;
31
32      try {
33        logfile.write(str + "\n");
34        logfile.flush();
35      } catch (IOException e) {
36        System.err.println("Error writing to log file.");
37      }
38    }
39  }
```

The Logger class simply opens a log file (reflector.log) and writes lines to the log file using a log() method. If the boolean logging is set to false, nothing will be logged.

8.3 Exercises

1. Try setting up a multicast tunnel between two nonmulticast-connected LANs. Then run another multicast program (such as mping) through the tunnel.

2. Try measuring the performance of the reflector program as it is forced to forward greater numbers of packets. At what point does it degrade? In what ways could performance be improved?

3. Implement a UNI_TO_UNI reflector. Does this mode actually offer any benefits?

chapter **9**

Summarizing Lessons Learned

Writing multicast applications can be both straightforward and painstaking. In truth, writing the code to open the sockets, send data, and receive data is easy once you have learned how (read this book). Therefore, we have attempted to summarize what has been covered by culling the key lessons and presenting them together in one place. This chapter is a list of the most important points to remember when writing applications that use multicast sockets.

1. Writing your first multicast application is straightforward in that you have very little to worry about beyond just getting the socket to work correctly. However, keep in mind that "straightforward" does not mean "easy"!

2. Trying to write a commercial-grade, multicast-based application requires that a programmer implement a significant amount of robustness. This robustness is not always easy, especially since much of the infrastructure and many of the rules are changing frequently. The best situations in which to implement multicast applications are controlled situations such as local LANs or enterprise networks.

3. The current state of deployment is such that there is likely to be a relatively small amount of end-to-end, native support for multicast. Therefore, when getting started, confine your applications to a local network, in particular, a set of machines that do not go through a router. Sometimes, even switches can cause trouble.

4. The APIs are constantly evolving, and so is the programming language support for them. Choose your programming language carefully and make sure it will support all the functionality you need. See Appendix B for a summary of features by language.

5. One socket characteristic that can be set is the Time-To-Live (TTL). With current protocols, you can set the TTL to 255 and rely on the network to do the right thing. If you are worried about privacy, you can use small TTLs to control the scope, but once a packet is sent into the network, there is no true guarantee of privacy.

6. Another option to try to provide some basic privacy is to use administrative scoping. But administrative scoping can vary from network to network, so be careful about how your

application will run in different places in the network. The bottom line is that if you need true privacy, encrypt the data!

7. Multicast continues to evolve. At every Internet Engineering Task Force (IETF), there are new proposals on how to improve multicast. There are mailing lists to join, such as IETF's MBONED working group (see *www.ietf.org/*) and the IP Multicast Initiative (IPMI). On these lists, you can ask questions about how to implement certain functions. It is worthwhile to pay attention to the latest developments.

8. Selecting a multicast group address can be a tough problem. The best solution is to rely on the user to give the application an address to use. Aside from this, the programmer's best option is to choose an address from an administrative range and test for collisions by looking for other multicast packets. But be aware of the hidden station problem: though collisions may not be occurring at one receiver, they may be occurring at others.

9. Any Source Multicast (ASM) is the service model that has existed since the inception of IP multicast. It assumes that the network will bring traffic from all sources to group members. Source Specific Multicast (SSM) greatly simplifies the network's responsibility by assuming the application will use some out-of-band mechanism to discover a group's source(s). As of the writing of this book, SSM is not yet widely deployed, but it is envisioned that it will become an important part of multicast in the Internet. The requirements for the application developer are, first, determine the group's sources and, second, pass this information to the host. Determining the source is likely to be easy since it can be learned the same way the multicast group address was learned (a Web hyperlink, a command line option, etc.). Passing source information to the host is done using new socket options that have recently been created. The challenge for the application programmer is to know whether ASM and/or SSM is supported and whether the particular host supports the necessary functionality.

10. Multicast is based on UDP sockets *only*. This means there are no transport-layer services other than port numbers (multiplexing/demultiplexing). TCP-style services such as connections, in-order delivery, reliability, and congestion control do not come automatically with multicast. In fact, reliability and congestion control are two functions made very difficult by the idea of one-to-many packet delivery.

   ■ Reliability is hard because it reduces effective transmission from one-to-many to one-to-one. In other words, if even a single group member loses a packet, the source must retransmit it. This means the source must keep track of every receiver and then keep track of every packet sent and whether every receiver has acknowledged it or not. Numerous strategies have been proposed in the *research* literature, but very few are simple enough to be implemented on the average programming project. The best way to deal with reliability is to avoid needing it!

   ■ Congestion control is even harder than reliability. TCP congestion control attempts to find the maximum–minimum bandwidth across the unicast path (i.e., the maximum amount of bandwidth that can be sent across the link in the path with the least capacity). Given that multicast builds a tree, there are likely to be numerous max–min bottlenecks. Again, as with reliability, the academic literature has numerous congestion control strategies for multicast, but none are easily implemented. The best way to deal with congestion control requirements is not to find an absolute solution but to simply try to be friendly to the network (e.g., if packet loss is detected, reduce the transmission rate). This may not necessarily be friendly to other TCP flows, but it is better than nothing. And, finally, trying to control congestion immediately raises the question of how to deal with a heterogeneous group (a group with some dial-up users, some broadband users, and other, higher-speed users).

11. The ability to handle multicast packets is not a ubiquitous service in the Internet. Therefore, not all hosts can receive multicast packets. A simple, application-layer solution to this problem is to use a reflector. While the reflector itself might be easy to implement, the harder question for the application programmer is how to provide a seamless service that allows the user to be unaware of the exact details on how packets are delivered. The challenge for the network administrator is to provide enough bandwidth to support the replication of potentially large data streams. Of course, deploying native multicast is always a solution!

appendix **A**

Multicast History and Protocols

While this book focuses on multicast from an application programmer and socket point of view, it is immensely helpful to understand a little bit about what happens inside the network. In this appendix, we briefly describe the two service models in greater detail and then back up and present a brief history of how multicast evolved to its current point.

A.1 Multicast Service Models

One of the most important facts to recognize is that there are currently two different service models. The first model, called Any Source Multicast (ASM), has been around since 1989 when RFC 1112 was published. Only with the advent of Source Specific Multicast (SSM), however, has there been a need to name the original model. ASM has a couple of recognized deficiencies. These deficiencies have resulted in more deployment complexities than most network operators are willing to tolerate. Therefore, for numerous reasons, multicast deployment has been slow. The result has been to rework the service model and create an alternative called SSM.

SSM removes the function of source discovery and moves it to the application layer. This simplifies the number of protocols needed *in* the network. The work to develop SSM began only recently. As of the date this book was published, SSM had not been accepted by the Internet Engineering Task Force (IETF) as a standard.[1] Therefore, in discussing these two service models, we have jumped forward in the history of multicast to the late 1990s. The next section will attempt to go back and trace the early history of multicast.

In order to understand the implications of the two different multicast service models, it is important to make a distinction between a *protocol architecture* and a *service model*. A multicast protocol architecture refers to a set of protocols that together allow end hosts to join/leave multicast groups, and it allows routers to communicate with each other to build

---

[1] For the record, IETF standards are called Request For Comments (RFCs). While this is a strange name for a standard, its naming is a result of the Internet's early evolution.

and forward data along inter-domain forwarding trees. An IP multicast service model refers to the semantics of the multicast service that a network provides an end user with. These services are provided to an end user at the application interface level. These services are made possible by the network protocol architecture. The basic characteristics of the service model include

- An application programming interface (API) used by applications to communicate with the host operating system
- Host operating system support for the API
- Protocol(s) used by the host operating system to communicate with the leaf network routers (referred to as designated routers or edge routers)
- Protocol(s) for building inter-domain multicast trees and for forwarding data along these trees

This list is ordered by what this book covers. The API for various languages and the implications of various operating systems are covered in this book. The network protocols used are only briefly mentioned here in the appendix, though numerous other books are available that cover these protocols in detail.

ASM and SSM are both derived from specific protocol architectures. While ASM and SSM have many similarities in the protocols they use in the backbone, the main difference is in the version of the Internet Group Management Protocol (IGMP). IGMP is used to communicate between the host operating system and the leaf router in the network. It is the protocol that exists just behind the socket interface visible to the application programmer.

ASM uses IGMPv2. In this service model, to become a member of a particular group, end hosts register their membership with a *querier router* that is responsible for handling multicast group membership functionality. Multicast-capable routers then construct a distribution tree by exchanging messages with each other according to a routing protocol. A number of different protocols exist for building multicast forwarding trees. These protocols differ mainly in the type of delivery tree constructed [11, 14, 18, 19, 1]. Of these, the Protocol Independent Multicast-Sparse Mode (PIM-SM) protocol [18, 19] is the most widely deployed in today's public networks. PIM-SM, by default, constructs a single spanning tree rooted at a core Rendezvous Point (RP) for all group members within a domain. Local sources then send their data to this RP, which forwards the data down the shared tree to interested local receivers. A receiver joining a host group can only specify interest in the entire group and therefore will receive data from any source sending to this group. Distribution via a shared tree can be effective for certain types of traffic (e.g., where the number of sources is large, since forwarding on the shared tree is performed via a single multicast forwarding entry). However, there are many cases (e.g., Internet broadcast streams) where forwarding from a source to a receiver is more efficient via the shortest path. PIM-SM also allows a designated router serving a particular subnet to switch to a source-based shortest path tree for a given source once the source's address is learned from data arriving on the shared tree. This capability provides for distribution of data from local sources to local receivers using a common RP inside a given PIM domain. PIM RPs can also learn about sources in other PIM domains by using the Multicast Source Discovery Protocol (MSDP) [27]. Once an active remote source is identified, an RP can join the shortest path tree to that source and obtain data to forward down the local shared tree on behalf of interested local receivers. Designated routers for particular subnets can again switch to a source-based shortest path tree for a given remote source once the source's address is learned from data arriving on the shared tree.

SSM uses IGMPv3. In this service model, to become a member of a particular group, end hosts still register their membership with the querier router, but now they must also specify the source address in addition to the group address. The SSM service model defines a *channel* as an (S,G) pair, where S is a source address and G is an SSM group address. Therefore, in this model, there is no need to use shared trees or implement any of the mechanisms to discover group sources. Whereas ASM discovers sources by a complex function of broadcast messages, SSM puts the burden on the application to explicitly identify the source or set of sources. IGMPv3 has the capability of carrying source information in its messages from the end host to the leaf router. Once the leaf router has this information, it sends a join along the reverse shortest path toward the source.

ASM and SSM can co-exist because the multicast address space has been divided into two regions. The SSM range is 232.0.0.0/8, and the ASM range is everything else in 224.0.0.0/4 that is not still reserved. Properly configured routers know to handle requests to join ASM and SSM groups differently. Luckily, very little additional complexity is needed for this. The operation is essentially for edge routers to know that for addresses in SSM the router should expect IGMPv3 messages that contain not only the group address but also the source address. Instead of forwarding these join requests to the RP, it should immediately send a reverse shortest path join toward the source. Otherwise, for ASM groups, the router should send a join request to the RP.

From a programmer's perspective, the question is whether to use the ASM or the SSM model. Assuming equal deployment (which as of this writing is not the case), the decision is determined based on the kind of application. If the application has a small set of static sources, then SSM is better. Examples of SSM applications include streaming media broadcasts from a well-known source, such as a broadcast of CNN. ASM is better suited when there is a need for a large number of sources *or* the source alternates between members of a set of different IP addresses.

Given that deployment can vary from no multicast support to ASM support only to ASM and SSM support, it becomes the responsibility of the application programmer to program robustness into the application. First, the programmer should test to see if there is support for SSM by testing the socket interface for passing source information to the operating system. If this does not exist, the application should then attempt to use ASM.

A.2 The Evolution of Multicast

We now turn our attention to the evolution of multicast from its inception in the early 1990s until the development of SSM in the late 1990s. From the first Internet-wide experiments in 1992 to the middle of 1997, standardization and deployment in multicast focused on a single flat topology. This topology is in contrast to the Internet topology, which is based on a hierarchical routing structure. The initial multicast protocol research and standardization efforts were aimed at developing routing protocols for this flat topology. Beginning in 1997, when the multicast community realized the need for a hierarchical multicast infrastructure and inter-domain routing, the existing protocols were categorized as intra-domain protocols and work began on standardizing an inter-domain solution.

A.2.1   Birth of the Multicast Backbone

Interest in building a multicast-capable Internet, motivated by Deering's work [12], began to achieve critical mass in the late 1980s. This work led to the creation of multicast in the Internet [11] and the creation of the multicast backbone (MBone) [9, 17]. In March 1992, the MBone carried its first worldwide event when 20 sites received audio from the meeting of the Internet Engineering Task Force (IETF) [10] in San Diego. While the conferencing software itself represented a considerable accomplishment, the most significant achievement here was the deployment of a virtual multicast network. The multicast routing function was provided by workstations running a daemon process called *mrouted*, which received unicast-encapsulated multicast packets on an incoming interface and then forwarded packets over the appropriate set of outgoing interfaces. Connectivity among these machines was provided using point-to-point, IP-encapsulated *tunnels*. Each tunnel connected two endpoints via one logical link but could cross several Internet routers. Once a packet is received, it could be sent to other tunnel endpoints or broadcast to local members. Routing decisions were made using the Distance Vector Multicast Routing Protocol (DVMRP) [37]. In this earliest phase of the MBone, all tunnels were terminated on workstations, and the MBone topology was such that sometimes multiple tunnels ran over a common physical link. Multicast routing in the early MBone was actually a controlled form of flooding. The first versions of *mrouted* did not implement pruning. Not until several years later was pruning deployed.

The original multicast routing protocol, DVMRP, creates multicast trees using a technique known as *broadcast and prune*. Because of the way the tree is constructed by DVMRP, it is called a *reverse shortest path tree*. The steps to creating this type of tree are as follows:

1. The source broadcasts each packet on its local network. An attached router receives the packet and sends it on all outgoing interfaces.

2. Each router that receives a packet performs a Reverse Path Forwarding (RPF) check. That is, each router checks to see if the incoming interface on which a multicast packet is received is the interface the router would use as an outgoing interface to reach the source. In this way, a router will choose to only receive packets on the one interface that it believes is the most efficient path back to the source. All packets received on the proper interface are forwarded on all outgoing interfaces. All others are discarded silently.[2]

3. Eventually, a packet will reach a router with some number of attached hosts. This *leaf router* will check to see if it knows of any group members on any of its attached subnets. A

---

[2] In reality, the action for a packet that fails an RPF check depends on the protocol. Some protocols tell all upstream routers except the RPF router to stop forwarding packets.

router discovers the existence of group members by periodically issuing Internet Group Management Protocol (IGMP) [8, 13, 20] queries. If there are members, the leaf router forwards the multicast packet on the subnet. Otherwise, the leaf router will send a *prune message* toward the source on the RPF interface (i.e., the interface the leaf router would use to forward packets to the source).

4. Prune packets are forwarded back toward the source, and routers along the way create prune state for the interface on which the prune message is received. If prune messages are received on all interfaces except the RPF interface, the router will send a prune message of its own toward the source.

In this way, reverse shortest path trees are created. These trees can be constructed even on a virtual topology like the MBone. Broadcast-and-prune protocols are also known as *dense mode* protocols because they are designed to perform best when the topology is densely populated with group members. Routers assume there are group members downstream and so forward packets. Only when explicit prune messages are received does a router not forward multicast traffic. If a group is densely populated, routers are unlikely to ever need to prune. The key disadvantage of dense mode protocols is that state information must be kept for *each* source at *every* router in the network, regardless of whether downstream group members exist. If a group is not densely populated, significant state must be stored in the network and a significant amount of bandwidth may be wasted.

A.2.2   Evolution of Intra-domain Multicast

Since 1992, the MBone has grown tremendously. It is no longer a simple virtual network sitting on top of the Internet but is rapidly becoming integrated into the Internet itself. In addition to simple DVMRP tunnels between workstations, the MBone now has *native* multicast capability (i.e., routers are capable of handling multicast packets). Furthermore, ongoing research has led to the development and deployment of two additional dense mode protocols. These are described next.

MOSPF

The protocol multicast extensions to OSPF (MOSPF) [30] uses the Open Shortest Path First (OSPF) [31] protocol to provide multicast. Basically, MOSPF routers flood an OSPF area with information about group receivers. This allows all MOSPF routers in an area to have the same view of group membership. In the same way that each OSPF router independently constructs the unicast routing topology, each MOSPF router can construct the shortest path tree for each source and group. While group membership reports are flooded throughout the OSPF area, data is not. MOSPF is something of an oddity in terms of classification. It is considered a dense mode protocol because membership information is broadcast to each MOSPF router, but it is also considered an explicit join protocol because data is sent only to those receivers that specifically request it. The key to understanding MOSPF is to realize that it is heavily dependent on OSPF and its link state routing paradigm.

PIM-DM

Protocol Independent Multicast (PIM) [14] has been split into two protocols, a dense mode version called PIM-DM [1] and a sparse mode version called PIM-SM [19]. PIM-DM is very similar to DVMRP; there are only two major differences. The first is that PIM (both dense mode and sparse mode) uses the unicast routing table to perform RPF checks. While DVMRP maintains its own routing table, PIM uses whatever unicast table is available. The name PIM is derived from the fact that the unicast table can be built using any unicast routing algorithm. PIM simply requires the unicast routing table to exist and so is *independent* of the algorithm used to build it. The second difference between PIM-DM and DVMRP is that DVMRP tries to avoid sending unnecessary packets to neighbors that will then generate prune messages based on a failed RPF check. The set of outgoing interfaces built by a given DVMRP router will include only those downstream routers that use the given router to reach the source (successful RPF check). PIM-DM avoids this complexity, but the trade-off is that packets are forwarded on all outgoing interfaces. Unnecessary packets are often forwarded to routers that must then generate prune messages because of the resulting RPF failure.

The next evolutionary step in intra-domain routing was to develop protocols that addressed the disadvantages of dense mode protocols. A new class of protocols, called *sparse mode* protocols, was created. Instead of optimizing only for the case when a group has many members, sparse mode protocols are designed to work more efficiently when there are only a few widely distributed group members. Instead of broadcasting traffic and triggering prune messages, receivers are expected to send explicit join messages. These join messages are sent to a router acting as a *core*. Sources are expected to send their data traffic to this same node. The use of a core as a "meeting place" for sources and receivers facilitates creation of the multicast tree. Two of the most popular sparse mode protocols are described next.

CBT

The Core-Based Trees (CBT) protocol was first discussed in the research community [5] and is now being standardized by the IETF [4]. CBT uses the basic sparse mode paradigm to create a single *shared tree* used by all sources. The tree is rooted at a core. All sources send their data to the core, and all receivers send explicit join messages to the core. There are two differences between CBT and PIM-SM. First, CBT uses only a shared tree and is not designed to use shortest path trees. Second, CBT uses *bidirectional* shared trees, but PIM-SM uses *unidirectional* shared trees. Bidirectional shared trees involve slightly more complexity but are more efficient when packets traveling from a source to the core cross branches of the multicast tree. In this case, instead of only sending traffic "up" to the core, packets can also be sent "down" the tree. While CBT has significant technical merits and is on a par technically with PIM-SM, few routing vendors provide support for CBT.

PIM-SM

PIM-SM [18, 19] is much more widely used than CBT. It is similar to PIM-DM in that routing decisions are based on whatever underlying unicast routing table exists, but the tree construction mechanism is quite different. PIM-SM's tree construction algorithm is actually more similar to that used by CBT than to that used by PIM-DM. In the following description of sparse mode protocol operation, we use PIM-SM as our example.

1. A core, called a rendezvous point (RP) in PIM terminology, must be configured.[3] Different groups may use different routers for RPs, but a group can have only a single RP.

   ■ Information about which routers in the network are RPs, and the mappings of multicast groups to RPs, must be discovered by all routers.

   ■ RP discovery is done using a bootstrap protocol. However, because the RP discovery mechanism is not included in the PIM-SMv1 specification, each vendor implementation of PIM-SMv1 has its own RP discovery mechanism. For PIM-SMv2, the bootstrap protocol is included in the protocol specification.

   ■ The basic function of the bootstrap protocol, in addition to RP discovery, is to provide robustness in case of RP failure. The bootstrap protocol includes mechanisms to select an alternate RP if the primary RP goes down.

2. Receivers send explicit *join messages* to the RP. Forwarding state is created in each router along the path from the receiver to the RP. A single shared tree, rooted at the RP, is formed for each group. As with other multicast protocols, the tree is a reverse shortest path tree—join messages follow a reverse path from receivers to the RP.

3. Each source sends multicast data packets, encapsulated in unicast packets, to the RP. When an RP receives one of these *register packets,* a number of actions are possible. First, if the RP has forwarding state for the group (i.e., there are receivers that have joined the group), the encapsulation is stripped off the packet and it is sent on the shared tree. However, if the RP does not have forwarding state for the group, it sends a *register stop message* to the RP. This avoids wasting bandwidth between the source and the RP. Second, the RP may wish to send a join message toward the source. By establishing multicast forwarding state between the source and the RP, the RP can receive the source's traffic as multicast and avoid the overhead of encapsulation.

These steps describe the basic mechanism used by sparse mode protocols in general and PIM-SM in particular. In summary, the basic goal is to use the RP as a "meeting place" for sources and receivers. Receivers explicitly join the shared tree, and sources register with the RP.

Sparse mode protocols have a number of advantages over dense mode protocols. First, sparse mode protocols typically offer better scalability in terms of routing state. Only routers on the path between a source and a group member must keep state. Dense mode protocols require state in all routers in the network. Second, sparse mode protocols are more efficient because the use of explicit join messages means multicast traffic only flows across links that have been explicitly added to the tree.

Sparse mode protocols do have a few disadvantages. These are mostly related to the use of RPs. First, the RP can be a single point of failure. Second, the RP can become a hot spot for

---

[3]Deciding how many RPs to have and where to place them in the network is a network planning issue and is beyond the scope of this book. A recent book offers some discussion on this topic [38].

multicast traffic. Third, having traffic forwarded from a source to the RP and then to receivers means that nonoptimal paths may exist in the multicast tree. The first problem is mostly solved with the bootstrap router protocol. The second and third problems are solved in CBT by using bidirectional trees. PIM-SM solves these problems by providing a mechanism to switch from a shared tree to a shortest path tree. This change occurs when a leaf router sends a special message toward the source. Forwarding state is changed so traffic flows directly to the receiver, instead of first through the RP. This action occurs when a traffic rate threshold is violated.

Finally, not only has progress been made in protocol development, but MBone growth has led to increased user awareness of multicast, which in turn has led to demand for new applications and better support for real-time data. Improvements have been made in transport-layer protocols. For example, the Real-Time Protocol (RTP) [33] assists loss- and delay-sensitive applications in adapting to the Internet's best-effort service model. With respect to applications, the MBone has seen an increasingly diverse set of media types. Originally, the MBone was considered a research effort, and its evolution was overseen by members of the MBone community. Coordination of events was handled almost exclusively through the use of a global session directory tool, originally called *sd* but now called *sdr*. As multicast deployment has continued, and as multicast has been integrated into the Internet as a native service, the informal use agreements and guidelines have faded. Even though *sdr*-based sessions remain at the core of Internet multicast events, their percentage of the total is shrinking. Other applications are being deployed that do not coordinate sessions through *sdr* or use RTP. This potpourri of tools has enriched the diversity of applications available, but it has stressed the ability of the network to provide multicast according to the standard IP multicast model.

For clarity, it is worth summarizing the key multicast terminology. Multicast protocols use either a *broadcast-and-prune* or an *explicit join* mechanism. Broadcast-and-prune protocols are commonly called dense mode protocols and always use a reverse shortest path tree rooted at a source. Explicit join protocols, commonly called sparse mode protocols, can use either a reverse shortest path tree or a *shared tree*. A shared tree uses a core or a rendezvous point to bring sources and receivers together.

A.2.3 Problems with Multicast

As the MBone has grown, it has suffered from an increasing number of problems, and these problems have been occurring with increasing frequency. The most important reason for this is the growing difficulty of managing a flat virtual topology. The same problems experienced with class-based unicast routing have manifested themselves in the MBone. As the MBone has grown, its size has become a problem, in terms of both routing state and susceptibility to misconfigurations. As a result, the multicast community has realized the need to deploy hierarchical, inter-domain routing. In particular, the MBone faces problems of scalability and manageability.

Scalability

Large, flat networks are inherently unstable. Exacerbating this problem are organizational mechanisms that do not provide significant route aggregation. For these two reasons, the

MBone has experienced substantial scalability problems. At its peak, the MBone had almost 10,000 routes. Unfortunately, most of these routes had long prefixes (between /28 and /32), which meant that very few hosts could be represented in each routing table entry. These scalability problems are not new. As the Internet has grown, unicast routing has had to be fundamentally changed to enable continued growth and stability. The solutions—route aggregation and hierarchical routing—have proved successful, and the issue now is how to apply them to multicast.

Manageability

As the MBone has grown, it has become harder to manage. The MBone has no central management, and most tasks have been handled on a per-site basis. Most coordination takes place via the MBone mailing list. Because the MBone is a virtual topology and new sites can be connected anywhere, there should be a formal procedure for adding new sites. Because no such mechanism exists, the MBone has grown randomly, and there are many inefficiencies. Two types of inefficiency commonly observed are the following:

- **Virtual Topology (Tunnel) Management:** The MBone is characterized as a set of multicast-capable islands connected by tunnels. The goal has always been to connect these islands in the most efficient manner, but over time suboptimal tunnels have been created. Tunnels are often set up in very inefficient ways. This behavior was observed very early in the history of the MBone, especially with regard to the MCI backbone. To avoid the growing tangle of tunnels, engineers at MCI undertook the difficult task of enforcing a policy that tunnels through or into the MCI network would have to be terminated at designated border points. The goal was to resolve the observed problem of single physical links being crossed by several (up to 10) tunnels. The work of the MCI engineers set an example that helped keep the MBone reasonably efficient for a number of years.

- **Inter-domain Policy Management:** Domain boundaries are another source of problems when trying to manage a flat topology. The model in today's Internet is to establish Autonomous System (AS) boundaries between Internet domains. ASs are commonly managed or owned by different organizations. Entities in one AS are typically not trusted by entities in another AS. As a result, exchange of routing information across AS boundaries is handled very carefully. Peering relationships among ASs are provisioned using the Border Gateway Protocol (BGP), which provides routing abstraction and policy control [25, 32, 36]. As a result of wide-scale use of BGP, there is a commonly accepted procedure when two ASs wish to communicate. Because the MBone does not provide such an inter-domain protocol, it offers no protection across domain boundaries. When there is a single flat topology connected using tunnels, routing problems can easily spread throughout the topology.

To summarize, the first problem is the complexity and instability of a large flat topology. The second problem is that there are no protocol mechanisms to build a hierarchical multicast routing topology. The need to solve these two problems created the first attempts to deploy inter-domain multicast.

A.2.4   Evolution of Inter-domain Multicast

Inter-domain multicast has evolved out of the need to provide scalable, hierarchical, Internet-wide multicast. Protocols that provide the necessary functionality have been developed, but the technology is relatively immature. These protocols are being considered by the IETF while being evaluated through extensive deployment. The particular inter-domain solution in use is considered near term and is possibly only an interim solution. Although the solution is functional, it lacks elegance and long-term scalability. As a result, additional work is under way to find long-term solutions. Some of these proposals are based on the standard IP multicast model. Others attempt to refine the service model in hopes of making the problem easier.

Inter-domain multicast routing has three parts. The first is a straightforward extension of the inter-domain unicast route exchange protocol BGP. The second and third are additional protocols needed to build and interconnect trees across domain boundaries.

Carrying Multicast Routes in BGP

The first requirement follows from the need to make multicast routing hierarchical in the same manner as unicast routing. Route aggregation and abstraction, as well as hop-by-hop policy routing, are provided in unicast using the Border Gateway Protocol (BGP) [32]. BGP offers substantial abstraction and control among domains. Within a domain, a network administrator can run any routing protocol desired. Routing to hosts in an external domain is simply a matter of choosing the best external link.

BGP supports inter-domain routing by reliably exchanging network reachability information. This information is used to compute an end-to-end distance vector–style path of AS numbers. Each AS advertises the set of routes it can reach and an associated cost. Each border router can then compute the set of ASs that should be traversed to reach any network. The use of a distance vector algorithm together with full path information allows BGP to overcome many of the limitations of traditional distance vector algorithms. Packets are still routed on a hop-by-hop basis, but less information is needed and better routing decisions can be made.

The functionality provided by BGP and its well-understood paradigm for connecting ASs are important catalysts for supporting inter-domain multicast. A version of BGP capable of carrying multicast routes not only would provide hierarchical routing and policy decisions, but also would allow a service provider to use different topologies for unicast and multicast traffic.

The mechanism by which BGP has been extended to carry multicast routes is called multiprotocol extensions to BGP4 (MBGP) [6].[4] MBGP is able to carry routes for multiple different protocols by adding the Subsequent Address Family Identifier (SAFI) to two BGP4 messages: MP_REACH_NLRI and MP_UNREACH_NLRI. Specifically for multicast, the SAFI field can specify unicast, multicast, or unicast/multicast. With MBGP, instead of every router needing to know the entire

---

[4] There is some ambiguity over terminology here. First, multiprotocol BGP4 is sometimes also referred to as BGP4+. Second, some think that MBGP stands for *multicast* BGP. All three terms refer to the same protocol.

flat multicast topology, each router needs to know only the topology of its own domain and the paths to reach each of the other domains.

There is some confusion over exactly what functionality MBGP provides. To be clear, we offer the following example. If one domain advertises reachability for multicast, the message will say, "I have a path to sources on the networks listed in this message." MBGP messages do not carry information about multicast groups (i.e., Class D addresses are never carried in an MBGP message). Recall that multicast trees are constructed using a reverse path back to the source. Therefore, MBGP information is used when a join message is sent from an RP or a receiver toward the source. This join message needs to know the best reverse path toward the source. MBGP provides this next-hop information between domains. If all unicast and multicast topologies were assumed to be the same, the reverse path join could simply follow the same next hop that any unicast traffic would follow. MBGP allows a network administrator to specify a different reverse path for the join to follow, and (subsequently) a different forward path when data is sent.

MBGP is the first step toward providing inter-domain multicast, but it alone is not a complete solution. MBGP is capable of determining the next hop to a host, but it is not capable of providing multicast tree construction functions. More specifically, what is the format of the join message? When should join messages be sent, and how often? Support for this functionality is not provided by MBGP; a true inter-domain multicast routing protocol is needed. Furthermore, conventional wisdom suggests that this protocol should not use the broadcast-and-prune method of tree construction. The near-term solution being advocated is to use PIM-SM to establish a multicast tree between domains containing group members.

The Multicast Source Discovery Protocol

To summarize, various intra-domain routing protocols exist, there is a route exchange protocol to support multicast, and PIM-SM is to be used to connect receivers and sources across domain boundaries. But there is still one function missing from the near-term solution. This function is needed when trying to connect sparse mode domains together. Given that PIM-SM is the only sparse mode protocol that has seen significant deployment, this function tends to be heavily influenced by PIM-SM. The problem is basically how to inform an RP in one domain that there are sources in other domains. The underlying assumption here is that a group can now have multiple RPs. However, the reality is that there is still only one RP per domain, but now multiple domains may be involved. The approach adopted is largely motivated by the perceived needs of the ISP community. In fact, the decision to have multiple RPs rather than a single root is what differentiates the near-term solution from other proposed solutions.

A problem arises when group members are spread over multiple domains. There is no mechanism to connect the various intra-domain multicast trees together. While traffic from all the sources for a particular group *within a particular domain* will reach the group's receivers, any sources outside the domain will remain disjoint. Why is this the case? Within a domain, receivers send join messages toward one RP and sources send register messages to the same RP. However, there is no way for an RP in one domain to find out about sources in other domains using different RPs. There is no mechanism for RPs to communicate with each other when one receives a source register message.

The decision to maintain a separate multicast tree and RP for each domain is driven by the need to reduce administrative dependencies between domains. Two potential problems are avoided in this way.

1. It is not necessary for two domains to co-administer a single sparse mode cloud. Relevant administrative functions include identifying candidate RPs and establishing the group RP mapping.

2. It becomes possible to avoid second- and third-party dependencies, in which multicast delivery for sources and groups in one or more domains is dependent on another domain whose only function is to provide the RP. Dependencies can occur when all sources and receivers in the RP's domain leave or become inactive. The domain with the RP has no group members and yet is still providing the RP service. Depending on how multicast and inter-domain traffic billing is handled, this could be particularly undesirable.

The near-term solution adopted for this problem is a new protocol, appropriately named the Multicast Source Discovery Protocol (MSDP) [27]. This protocol works by having representatives in each domain announce to other domains the existence of active sources. MSDP is run in the same router as a domain's RP (or one of the RPs). MSDP's operation is similar to that of MBGP, in that MSDP sessions are configured between domains and TCP is used for reliable session message exchange. We describe MSDP operation next.

1. When a new source for a group becomes active, it will register with the domain's RP.

2. The MSDP peer in the domain will detect the existence of the new source and send a Source Active (SA) message to all directly connected MSDP peers.

3. MSDP message flooding:
   - MSDP peers that receive an SA message will perform a *peer RPF check*. The MSDP peer that received the SA message will check to see if the MSDP peer that sent the message is along the "correct" MSDP peer path. These peer RPF checks are necessary to prevent SA message looping.
   - If an MSDP peer receives an SA message on the correct interface, the message is forwarded to all MSDP peers except the one from which the message was received. This is called *peer RPF flooding*.

4. Within a domain, an MSDP peer (also the RP) will check to see if it has state for any group members in the domain. If state does exist, the RP will send a PIM join message to the source address advertised in the SA message.

5. If data is contained in the message, the RP then forwards it on the multicast tree. Once group members receive data, they may choose to switch to a shortest path tree using PIM-SM conventions.

6. Steps 3–5 are repeated until all MSDP peers have received the SA message and all group members are receiving data from the source.

This ends the description of the short-term inter-domain multicast routing solution. The solution is referred to with the abbreviations for the three relevant protocols: MBGP/

PIM-SM/MSDP. However, while the given description is relatively complete, there are a number of details that are not discussed. And, as with any system, most of the complexity is in the details. Furthermore, we have not yet discussed the limitations of the current solution in any detail. In particular, a qualitative assessment of the scalability, complexity, and overall quality of the protocols would be valuable.

The MBGP/PIM-SM/MSDP solution is relatively straightforward once a person understands all the abbreviations and understands the motivating factors that drove the design of the protocols. While some argue that the current set of protocols is not simple, it really is no more complex than many other Internet services, such as unicast routing. The key advantage of MBGP/PIM-SM/MSDP is that it is a functional solution largely built on existing protocols. Furthermore, it is already being deployed with a fair amount of success. The key disadvantage is that, as a long-term solution, the MBGP/PIM-SM/MSDP protocol suite may be susceptible to scalability problems.

appendix **B**

Summary of Multicast API by Language

This appendix provides a quick guide to the multicast functions and methods by programming language. Table B.1 is divided into four columns: C, Java, the C# Socket class, and the C# UdpClient class. For each multicast-related feature, the appropriate function or class/method is listed. For any feature that is not implemented for that language, the column is marked as nonapplicable (n/a).

The primary difference in the APIs is that Java does not currently have SSM support yet, although as SSM becomes more common Java support will undoubtedly follow. The Java address checking methods are useful and unique to Java but would have been easily implemented by a programmer. The C# Socket API is a thinly veiled wrapper of the nearly identical C API, while Java hides some of the ugliness of the setsockopt() overloading. The C# UdpClient class is a very bare-bones subset of multicast functionality.

Table B.1

FEATURE	C	Java	C# Socket	C# UdpClient
Create socket	socket()	MulticastSocket()	Socket()	UdpClient()
Close socket	close()	MulticastSocket.close()	Socket.Close()	UdpClient.Close()
Set TTL	setsockopt()	MulticastSocket.setTimeToLive() MulticastSocket.setTTL()	Socket.SetSocketOption()	UdpClient.JoinMulticastGroup()
Get TTL	getsockopt()	MulticastSocket.getTimeToLive() MulticastSocket.getTTL()	Socket.GetSocketOption()	n/a
Set loopback	setsockopt()	MulticastSocket.setLoopback()	Socket.SetSocketOption()	n/a
Get loopback	getsockopt()	MulticastSocket.getLoopback()	Socket.GetSocketOption()	n/a
Set interface	setsockopt()	MulticastSocket.setNetworkInterface()	Socket.SetSocketOption()	n/a
Get interface	getsockopt()	MulticastSocket.getNetworkInterface()	Socket.GetSocketOption()	n/a
Send packet	sendto()	MulticastSocket.send()	Socket.Send()	UdpClient.Send()
Set address reuse	setsockopt()	MulticastSocket.setReuseAddress()	Socket.SetSocketOption()	n/a
Bind socket	bind()	*(implicit)*	Socket.Bind()	n/a
Join group / add membership	setsockopt()	MulticastSocket.joinGroup()	Socket.SetSocketOption()	UdpClient.JoinMulticastGroup()
Receive packet	recvfrom()	MulticastSocket.receive()	Socket.ReceiveFrom()	UdpClient.Receive()
Leave group / drop membership	setsockopt()	MulticastSocket.leaveGroup()	Socket.SetSocketOption()	UdpClient.DropMulticastGroup()
SSM add source membership	setsockopt() ioctl()	n/a	Socket.SetSocketOption()	n/a
SSM drop source membership	setsockopt() ioctl()	n/a	Socket.SetSocketOption()	n/a
SSM block source	setsockopt() ioctl()	n/a	Socket.SetSocketOption()	n/a

FEATURE	C	Java	C# Socket	C# UdpClient
SSM unblock source	setsockopt() ioctl()	n/a	Socket.SetSocketOption()	n/a
Check multicast membership	n/a	InetAddress.isMulticastAddress()	n/a	n/a
Check global scope address	n/a	InetAddress.isMCGlobal()	n/a	n/a
Check link local scope address	n/a	InetAddress.isMCLinkLocal()	n/a	n/a
Check site local scope address	n/a	InetAddress.isMCSiteLocal()	n/a	n/a
Check org local scope address	n/a	InetAddress.isMCOrgLocal()	n/a	n/a

References

[1] A. Adams, J. Nicholas, and W. Siadak. Protocol independent multicast—dense mode (pim-dm): Protocol specification (revised). Internet Engineering Task Force (IETF) Internet Draft, draft-ietf-pim-dm-new-v2-*.txt, February 2002.

[2] Z. Albanna, K. Almeroth, D. Meyer, and M. Schipper. Iana guidelines for ipv4 multicast address assignments. Internet Engineering Task Force (IETF) RFC 3171, August 2001.

[3] K. Almeroth, S. Bhattacharyya, and C. Diot. Challenges of integrating asm and ssm ip multicast protocol architectures. In *International Workshop on Digital Communications: Evolutionary Trends of the Internet (IWDC '01)*, Taormina, Italy, September 2001.

[4] A. Ballardie. Core based trees (CBT version 2) multicast routing. Internet Engineering Task Force (IETF) RFC 2189, September 1997.

[5] T. Ballardie, P. Francis, and J. Crowcroft. Core based trees (CBT): An architecture for scalable multicast routing. In *ACM Sigcomm*, pages 85–95, San Francisco, September 1995.

[6] T. Bates, R. Chandra, D. Katz, and Y. Rekhter. Multiprotocol extensions for BGP-4. Internet Engineering Task Force (IETF) RFC 2283, February 1998.

[7] R. Braden. Requirements for Internet hosts—communication layers. Internet Engineering Task Force (IETF) RFC 1122, October 1989.

[8] B. Cain, S. Deering, B. Fenner, I. Kouvelas, and A. Thyagarajan. Internet group management protocol, version 3. Internet Engineering Task Force (IETF) Internet Draft, draft-ietf-idmr-igmp-v3-*.txt, January 2002.

[9] S. Casner. *Frequently Asked Questions (FAQ) on the Multicast Backbone (MBone)*. USC/ISI, December 1994. Available from *ftp://ftp.isi.edu/mbone/faq.txt*.

[10] S. Casner and S. Deering. First IETF Internet audiocast. *ACM Computer Communication Review*, pages 92–97, July 1992.

[11] S. Deering. Host extensions for IP multicasting. Internet Engineering Task Force (IETF) RFC 1112, August 1989.

[12] S. Deering. Multicast routing in a datagram internetwork. Ph.D. Dissertation, 1991.

[13] S. Deering and D. Cheriton. Multicast routing in datagram internetworks and extended LANs. *ACM Transactions on Computer Systems*, pages 85–111, May 1990.

[14] S. Deering, D. Estrin, D. Farinacci, V. Jacobson, G. Liu, and L. Wei. PIM architecture for wide-area multicast routing. *IEEE/ACM Transactions on Networking*, pages 153–162, April 1996.

[15] C. Diot, B. Lyles, B. Levine, and H. Kassem. Requirements for the definition of new IP-multicast services. *IEEE Network*, pages 78–88, January/February 2000.

[16] M. J. Donahoo and K. L. Calvert. *The Pocket Guide to TCP/IP Sockets—C Version*. Morgan Kaufmann, San Francisco, 2001.

[17] H. Eriksson. The multicast backbone. *Communications of the ACM*, 8:54–60, August 1994.

[18] D. Estrin, D. Farinacci, A. Helmy, D. Thaler, S. Deering, M. Handley, V. Jacobson, C. Liu, P. Sharma, and L. Wei. Protocol independent multicast sparse-mode (PIM-SM): Protocol specification. Internet Engineering Task Force (IETF) RFC 2362, June 1998.

[19] B. Fenner, M. Handley, H. Holbrook, and I. Kouvelas. Protocol independent multicast—sparse mode (PIM-SM): Protocol specification (revised). Internet Engineering Task Force (IETF) Internet Draft, draft-ietf-pim-sm-v2-new-*.txt, March 2002.

[20] W. Fenner. Internet group management protocol, version 2. Internet Engineering Task Force (IETF) RFC 2236, November 1997.

[21] M. Handley. SAP: Session announcement protocol. Internet Engineering Task Force (IETF), draft-ietf-mmusic-sap-*.txt, March 2000.

[22] M. Handley and V. Jacobson. SDP: Session description protocol. Internet Engineering Task Force (IETF) RFC 2327, April 1998.

[23] H. Holbrook and B. Cain. Using igmpv3 for source-specific multicast. Internet Engineering Task Force (IETF) Internet Draft, draft-holbrook-idmr-igmpv3-ssm-*.txt, March 2000.

[24] H. Holbrook and B. Cain. Source-specific multicast for ip. Internet Engineering Task Force (IETF) Internet Draft, draft-ietf-ssm-arch-*.txt, November 2001.

[25] C. Huitema. *Routing in the Internet*. Prentice Hall, Englewood Cliffs, New Jersey, 1995.

[26] D. Meyer. Administratively scoped ip multicast. Internet Engineering Task Force (IETF) RFC 2365, July 1998.

[27] D. Meyer and B. Fenner. Multicast source discovery protocol (MSDP). Internet Engineering Task Force (IETF) Internet Draft, draft-ietf-msdp-spec-*.txt, November 2001.

[28] D. Meyer and P. Lothberg. GLOP addressing in 233/8. Internet Engineering Task Force (IETF) RFC 2770, September 2001.

[29] C. K. Miller. *Multicast Networking and Applications*. Addison-Wesley, Reading, Massachusetts, 1998.

[30] J. Moy. Multicast extensions to OSPF. Internet Engineering Task Force (IETF) RFC 1584, March 1994.

[31] J. Moy. OSPF version 2. Internet Engineering Task Force (IETF) RFC 2178, April 1998.

[32] Y. Rekhter and T. Li. A border gateway protocol 4 (BGP-4). Internet Engineering Task Force (IETF) RFC 1771, March 1995.

[33] H. Schulzrinne, S. Casner, R. Frederick, and V. Jacobson. RTP: A transport protocol for real-time applications. Internet Engineering Task Force (IETF) RFC 1889, January 1996.

[34] W. R. Stevens. *Unix Network Programming Volume 1, Networking APIs: Sockets and XTI*. Prentice Hall PTR, Upper Saddle River, New Jersey, 1998.

[35] D. Thaler, B. Fenner, and B. Quinn. Socket interface extensions for multicast source filters. Internet Engineering Task Force (IETF) Internet Draft, draft-ietf-idmr-msf-api-*.txt, February 2000.

[36] P. Traina. Experience with the BGP-4 protocol. Internet Engineering Task Force (IETF) RFC 1773, March 1995.

[37] D. Waitzman, C. Partridge, and S. Deering. Distance vector multicast routing protocol (DVMRP). Internet Engineering Task Force (IETF) RFC 1075, November 1988.

[38] B. Williamson. *Developing IP Multicast Networks, Volume I (Fundamentals)*. Cisco Press, Indianapolis, Indiana, 1999.

Index

abstraction provided by sockets, 1
address collision avoidance, 79
Address Resolution Protocol (ARP), 6
address reuse option
  C#, 62-63, 69
  C programming language, 23-24
  Java, 43
  .NET, 62-63, 69
address selection, 92-93, 152
address specification
  big-endian/little-endian problem,
    14-15
  C#, 55-56, 60
  C programming language, 12-15,
    20
  Class D IP addresses, 13
  factors in, 13
  host order, 14-15
  Java, 35-36, 40, 48
  multicast address space, selecting
    from, 92-93, 152
  network order, 14-15
  populating address structures
    in C, 12-14, 20, 25, 30
addresses
  ASM range, 157
  checking scope, 171
  collision avoidance, 79
  multicast address space, 13, 90-93
  reuse. *See* address reuse option
  scope ranges, 89-90
  selecting for transmission, 92-93,
    152
  specification. *See* address
    specification
  SSM range, 92, 157
Address.java, 130-131
administrative scoping, 89-90,
  151-152
advantages of multicast, 1, ix
all-hosts group, 96
all-routers group, 96
any source option, 81
APIs (Application Programming
  Interfaces)
  C. *See* C programming language
  C#. *See* C# programming language
  Java. *See* Java
  nature of sockets, 9
  .NET. *See* .NET platform
  UDP, 9-10
application programmers, goal for,
  ix-x
application-layer multicast
  advantages of, 128
  defined, 127
  MBone. *See* MBone (Multicast
    Backbone)
  network-layer multicast, compared
    to, 127-128
  reflectors. *See* reflectors

application-level congestion control,
  114-116
ARP (Address Resolution Protocol), 6
AS (Autonomous System) boundaries,
  163-164
ASM (Any Source Multicast)
  C# for, 70
  C programming for, 31
  deficiencies, 155
  IGMP with, 156
  protocol architectures, 156
  range of addresses for, 157
  (source, group) pair notation, 78
  SSM, compared to, 77-78
  summary, 152
Autonomous System (AS) boundaries,
  163-164

BGP (Border Gateway Protocol),
  163-165
bidirectional shared trees, 160
big-endian/little-endian problem,
  14-15
binding sockets
  C#, 63-64
  C programming language, 24, 30
  mping.c, 102-103
  programming languages
    compared, 170
  purpose of, 10
Border Gateway Protocol (BGP),
  163-165
broadcast
  defined, 2
  LAN use of, 3
  protocols formerly used, 87
broadcast-and-prune technique,
  158-159
broadcast-and-prune protocols, 87,
  159, 162

C programming language
  adding multicast membership, 24,
    30
  address reuse option, 23-24, 30
  address specification, 12-15, 20,
    30
  addresses for listening, 25
  advanced SSM API, 82-84
  any source option, 81
  arguments for multicast sockets,
    20
  binding addresses to sockets, 24,
    30
  closing sockets, 12, 23
  controlled source option, 81-82
  delta-based API, 80-82
  dotted quad notation, converting,
    14
  dropping membership, 26, 30
  filtering sources, 83

full-state SSM API, 82-84
getting socket options, 15-16
header files for socket creation,
  11, 20, 29, 31
host order, 14-15
interface options, 20-21
Internet family addresses, 11, 13
ioctl() function, 82-84
joining multicast groups, 24-26
loopback option, 21-22
mcreceive.c sample program,
  27-31
mcsend.c sample program, 18-20,
  30-31
mping.c. *See* mping.c sample
  program
multicast sender code, 18-20
multihomed host interface
  options, 21
multiple multicasts, listening to,
  25, 30
pinging with. *See* mping.c sample
  program
populating address structures,
  12-14, 20, 25, 30
port fields, 13, 20, 29
protocol selection, 11
receiver sample program, 27-30
receiving, function for, 26
receiving multicast packets, 22-30
return values, socket calls, 12
reuse address option, 23-24, 30
sending packets, 17, 20
setting socket options, 15-16
sockaddr data structure, 12
socket creation, 11-12, 20, 23, 30
SSM support, 80-84
steps for receiving multicast
  packets, 22, 27
steps for sending multicast
  packets, 10-11
TTL, 15-17, 20
UDP sockets, 9-10
Winsock modifications, 31-32
C# programming language
  adding membership, 64-65, 70,
    72-73
  address reuse option, 62-63, 69
  address specification, 55-56, 60,
    65
  arguments for Socket(), 53, 69
  ASM (Any Source Multicast), 70
  binding addresses to sockets,
    63-64
  closing sockets, 61, 70, 72
  connections, UdpClient, 72
  constants for, 53, 69
  dropping membership, 66, 70,
    72-73
  endpoints, 63-66, 69-70
  interface option, 64, 69

libraries, using, 52, 60, 69
MCReceive.cs sample program,
    66–70
MCSend.cs sample program, 58–61,
    70
namespace specification, 52, 60,
    69
options, retrieving values of,
    54–55, 62
options, setting, 53–54, 62, 64
populating datagram packets,
    56–57
port specification, 55–56, 60, 69
ports, binding addresses to, 63–64
ReceiveFrom() method, 65, 70
receiving multicast packets, 61–70,
    74
reuse option, 62–63, 69
Send() method, UdpClient class, 74
sending multicast packets, 52–61,
    74
SendTo() method, 57–58, 60
socket creation, 52–53, 60, 62, 69,
    71–72
SSM (Source Specific Multicast),
    70–71
steps for receiving multicast
    packets, 61–62, 67
steps for sending multicast
    packets, 52, 58
TTL, 53–55, 60, 73
UdpClient class, 51–52, 71–76
CBT (Core-Based Trees) protocol, 160
challenges to multicast, xi
channels, 78, 157
Class D IP addresses, 13
closing sockets
    C programs, 12, 20, 23
    C# programs, 61, 70
    Java programs, 34–35, 40
    mping.c, 112
    programming languages
        compared, 170
collision avoidance, 79
commercial-grade applications, 151
complexity, 3–4
congestion control
    application-level, 114–116
    design notes, 125–126
    group size estimation, 125–126
    hidden station problem, 125–126
    Internet Robustness Principle, 115
    mping.c implementation of,
        116–126
    NAK (negative acknowledgment)
        schemes, 115
    need for, 4
    random delays for, 115–117
    rate-limiting transmission,
        114–115
    RTP/RTCP, 115–116
    summary, 152–153
    TCP, 114
    UDP, adding to, 4, 114–115
connectivity, ensuring, 5
controlled source option, 81–82
Core-Based Trees (CBT) protocol, 160

cores, 160–161
creating sockets
    C#, 52–53, 62
    C programming, 11–12, 20, 23, 30
    Java, 34–36
    mping.c, 102–103
    .NET, 52–53, 62
    programming languages
        compared, 170
    Winsock, 31–32

definition of multicast, 2–3
delay sensitivity, 4
dense-mode protocols, 87–88, 159,
    161
deployment of multicast over
    Internet, 2, 151. See also
    network-layer multicast
disadvantages of multicast, xi
distance vector algorithms, 164
Distance Vector Multicast Routing
    Protocol (DVMRP), 87, 158
distribution trees. See forwarding
    trees
domain boundary problem, 163. See
    also inter-domain multicast
dotted quad notation, converting, 14
dropping membership
    C#, 66, 73
    C programming language, 26
    controlled source option in SSM,
        81–82
    Java, 45–46, 49
    mping.c example, 112
    programming languages
        compared, 170
DVMRP (Distance Vector Multicast
    Routing Protocol), 87, 158

evolution of multicast. See history of
    multicast
explicit join mechanisms, 162

feedback, scalable, 4–5
filtering sources, 79
firewalls, UDP blocked at, 4
forwarding trees
    branch formation, 25, 30
    cores, 160–161
    grafting, 6
    join messages, 44, 48
    protocols for, 156
    pruning, 6, 26, 30, 66, 158–159
    purpose of, 2
    reverse shortest path trees,
        158–159
    RPs, 79–80, 156–157, 161–162,
        165–166
    shared trees, 160
    shortest paths, 156–157
    steps in creating, 5–6

globally scoped addresses, 90, 93
GLOP range, 92
goal for application programmers,
    ix–x

grafting, 6
group membership. See membership
    in multicast groups, adding

hidden station problem, 125–126,
    152
hierarchical routing problem, 164
history of multicast
    BGP, 163–165
    broadcast and prune, 158–159
    CBT protocol, 160
    creation of multicast, 5, 158
    DVMRP, 158
    inter-domain multicast, 164–167
    intra-domain multicast, 159–162
    MBone creation, 158
    MBone, problems with, 162–163
    MOSPF, 159
    mrouted, 158
    MSDP, 165–167
    PIM-DM, 160
    PIM-SM, 160–162
    pruning, 158–159
    sparse mode, 160–161
    topologies, 157–158
    tunneling, 158
hops, number allowed. See TTL
    (Time-To-Live)
host order, 14–15

ICMP (Internet Control Message
    Protocol), 89
IETF (Internet Engineering Task
    Force), 152
IGMP (Internet Group Management
    Protocol)
    adding membership in C, 25
    ASM vs. SSM versions, 156–157
    discovery of members, 159
    join messages, from Java, 44
    leave messages, 26
    purpose of, 5–6
    SSM with, 79, 80
    version 3, 80, 157
infrastructure reduction by SSM,
    79–80
inter-domain multicast, 164–167
inter-domain policy management,
    163
interface options
    C#, 64, 69
    C programming language, 20–21
    Java, 40–42
    programming languages
        compared, 170
Internet Control Message Protocol
    (ICMP), 89
Internet Engineering Task Force
    (IETF), 152
Internet Group Management Protocol.
    See IGMP (Internet Group
    Management Protocol)
Internet Robustness Principle, 115
intra-domain multicast history,
    159–162

IP addresses. *See also* addresses
  adding to multicast groups. *See*
    membership in multicast
    groups, adding
  big-endian/little-endian problem,
    14–15
  C sockets, 12–15, 20
  dotted quad notation, converting,
    14
  host order, 14–15
  multicast address space, 90–93
  reusing. *See* address reuse option
  scope ranges, 89–90
  selection for multicast, 92–93, 152
  specifying. *See* address
    specification

Java
  adding membership, 44, 48
  address reuse option, 43
  address selection, 93–94
  address specification, 35–36, 40,
    48
  address structure, 35
  API, MulticastSocket, 33–34,
    170–171
  buffering, 48
  C, relationship to, 33
  closing sockets, 34–35, 40, 46, 49
  DatagramPacket constructors, 36
  dropping membership, 45–46, 49
  functions, table of, 170–171
  interface options, 40–42
  java.net package, 33
  join requests, 44, 48
  loopback options, 42
  mcreceive.java sample program,
    46–49
  mcsend.java sample program,
    38–40, 49
  membership, adding to, 44, 48
  metadata from packets, 45
  MulticastSocket API, 33–34,
    170–171
  MulticastSocket class, 37, 41, 43,
    46, 48–49
  network interface object definition,
    41–42
  packet creation, 36, 40
  ports, validating, 40, 48
  receiving, method for, 44–45
  receiving multicasts, 42–49
  reflector projects. *See*
    Reflector.java sample
    program
  reuse option, 43
  scope control methods, 93–94
  send() method, 37, 40
  sender program, 38–40
  sending multicasts, 34–42
  sending packets, 37, 40
  socket creation for receiving,
    42–43, 48
  socket creation for sending, 34–36,
    40
  SSM support lacking, 80

steps for receiving multicasts,
  42–43, 46
steps for sending multicasts, 34
testing for multicast addresses, 35
TTL, setting, 37, 40
version dependence, 33–34, 37, 43
join messages, 161
join-and-graft protocols, 88
joining multicast groups. *See*
  membership in multicast
  groups, adding

lack of support for multicast, xi
leaf routers, 5, 158–159
leaving groups. *See* dropping
  membership
link local scope, 90
listening. *See* receiving multicasts
local scope range, 89–90, 93
loopback option
  C programming language, 21–22
  C#, 61
  Java, 42
  programming languages
    compared, 170
lost packets, UDP treatment of, 10

mailing lists about multicast, 152
manageability issues, 163
MBGP (multiprotocol extensions to
  BGP4), 164–165
MBone (Multicast Backbone)
  application-layer nature of, 127
  creation of, 5, 158–159
  deficiencies of, 162–163
mcreceive.c sample program, 27–31
MCReceive.cs sample program, 66–70
mcreceive.java sample program,
  46–49
mcsend.c sample program, 18–20,
  30–31
MCSend.cs sample program, 58–61, 70
mcsend.java sample program, 38–40,
  49
membership, checking, 171
membership in multicast groups,
  adding
  C#, 64, 70
  C programming, 24–25, 30
  explicit join mechanisms, 162
  Java, 44, 48
  mping.c, 104
  .NET, 64, 70
  programming languages
    compared, 170
  (source, group) pair notation, 78
  UdpClient class, C#, 73
membership in multicast groups,
  dropping
  C#, 66, 73
  C programming, 26
  controlled source option in SSM,
    81–82
  Java, 45–46, 49
  mping.c, 112

programming languages
  compared, 170
UdpClient class, C#, 73
Microsoft .NET. *See* .NET platform
MOSPF (Multicast Open Shortest Path
  First), 159
mping.c sample program
  bandwidth limit, setting, 117
  check_send(), 121–122
  clean_exit(), 112
  congestion control for, 116–126
  get_local_host_info(), 104
  header file, 98–100
  init_socket(), 102–104
  main(), 100–102, 117–118
  packet construction, 104–105
  packet structure, 99–100, 116
  process_mping_packet(), 108–110
  received_packet_count(), 120–121
  receiver-based congestion control
    for, 116–126
  receiver_listen_loop(), 110–111,
    118–119
  response buffer, 116–117, 119–
    120
  running, 112–113
  running congestion control
    version, 123–124
  scalability of, 113–114
  sender_listen_loop(), 106–108,
    122–123
  send_interval(), 120
  send_mping(), 104–105
  send_packet(), 106
  socket creation, 102–104
  subtract_timeval(), 108
  timeval_to_ms(), 108
  usage(), 101–102
  validity of packets, checking,
    108–110
mrouted, 5, 129, 158
MSDP (Multicast Source Discover
  Protocol), 156, 165–167
multicast address space
  ASM range, 157
  categories, table of, 91
  Class D IP addresses, 13
  GLOP range, 92
  Java methods for, 92
  overview, 90–93
  sdr (session directory) tool, 91
  selecting, 92–93, 152
  SSM range, 92, 157
Multicast Backbone. *See* MBone
  (Multicast Backbone)
multicast forwarding trees. *See*
  forwarding trees
Multicast Open Shortest Path First
  (MOSPF), 159
multicast reflectors. *See* reflectors
Multicast Source Discover Protocol
  (MSDP), 156, 165–167
multihomed host interface options,
  20–21, 40–42, 64, 69
multiple multicasts, listening to, 25
multiprotocol extensions to BGP4
  (MBGP), 164–165

NAK (negative acknowledgment)
schemes, 115
native multicast, 127-128, 159
necessity of multicast, 1
negative acknowledgment (NAK)
schemes, 115
.NET platform
adding membership, 64-65
address reuse option, 62-63, 69
address specification, 55-56, 60
binding addresses to sockets,
63-64
C# programming. *See* C#
programming language
closing sockets, 61
cross-language support, 51-52
defined, 51
dropping membership, 66
IGMP v3 support, 80
languages supported, 51-52
MCReceive.cs sample program,
66-70
MCSend.cs sample program, 58-61,
70
namespace specification, 52, 60
populating datagram packets,
56-57
port validation, 55-56, 60
ReceiveFrom() method, 65
receiving multicast packets, 61-70
sending multicast packets, 52-61
socket creation, 52-53, 60, 62, 69
Sockets class, 52
sources, controlling, 84-85
SSM with, 84-85
steps for receiving multicast
packets, 61-62, 67
steps for sending multicast
packets, 52, 58
TTL, 53-55, 60
UdpClient class, 51-52, 71-76
network-layer multicast, 127-128

Open Shortest Path First (OSPF), 159
organizational local scope, 90
OSPF (Open Shortest Path First), 159

packet creation
C#, 56-57
Java, 36
mping.c, 99-100, 104-105, 1116
peer RFP flooding, 166
PIM-DM (Protocol Independent
Multicast-Dense Mode), 87, 160
PIM-SM (Protocol Independent
Multicast-Sparse Mode), 156,
160-162, 165
pinging
all-hosts group, 96
all-routers group, 96
congestion control for, mping.c,
116-126
get_local_host_info(), mping.c,
104
header file for mping.c, 98-100
main(), mping.c, 100-102

mping.c. *See* mping.c sample
program
multicast support for, 96-97
packet construction, 104-105
packet structure of mping.c,
99-100
process_mping_packet(), mping.c,
108-110
receiver_listen_loop(), mping.c,
110-111
running mping.c, 112-113
sender_listen_loop(), mping.c,
106-108
sending from mping.c, 104-105
send_packet(), mping.c, 106
time of round-trip, calculating,
107-108
unicast, 95-96
usage(), mping.c, 101-102
validity of packets, checking,
108-110
populating address structures
C programming language, 12-14,
20, 25, 30
mping.c, 102-103
populating packets
C#, 56-57
Java, 36
port numbers
Address.java, 130-131
C sockets, specifying in, 13
C#, specifying in, 55-56, 60, 69
Java, specifying in, 36, 43
purpose of, 1
validation, 29, 40, 48
programming languages with sockets
APIs, 9
Protocol Independent Multicast-
Sparse Mode (PIM-SM), 156,
160-162, 165
Protocol Independent Multicast-
Dense Mode (PIM-DM), 87,
160
protocols, multicast
BGP, 163-165
CBT, 160
DVMRP, 87, 158
ICMP, 89
IGMP. *See* IGMP (Internet Group
Management Protocol)
MBGP, 164-165
MSDP, 156, 165-167
overview, 5-6
RTP/RTCP, 115-116
UDP. *See* UDP (User Datagram
Protocol)
pruning, 6, 26, 30, 66, 158-159. *See
also* dropping membership
purpose of multicast, 2

querier routers, 156

ranges of multicast address space, 91
reachability
BGP exchange of information on,
164
flow, high level, mping.c, 100-102

header file for mping.c, 98-100
main(), mping.c, 100-102
mping, purpose of, 97-98
packet structure of mping.c,
99-100
problems with multicast, 96-97
unicast, 95-96
Real-Time Transport Control Protocol
(RTCP), 115-116
Real-Time Transport Protocol (RTP),
115-116, 162
receiving multicasts
addresses to join, setting, 25
C#, 61-70, 74
C programming language, 22-30
Java, 42-49
listening threads, 141-145
mcreceive.c sample program,
27-30
MCReceive.cs sample program,
66-70
mcreceive.java sample program,
46-49
overview, 10
programming languages
compared, 170
receiver_listen_loop(), mping.c,
110-111
ReflectorListener.java class,
142-145
sender_listen_loop(), mping.c,
106-108
steps for, 22, 42-43
Reflector.java sample program
Address.java, 130-131
architecture of, 129
code for, 131-140
configuration file, 140-142
DatagramSocket base class, 145
design of, 128
destination IP addresses, 141
listening threads, 141-145
Logger.java, 148-149
main(), 140
modes of, 128, 141
packet arrival events, 145
PacketListenerInterface.java,
141, 147
Reflector class, 140-141
ReflectorListener.java, 142-145
ReflectorSender.java, 145-148
scalability of, 128-129
sender class, 145-148
source IP address for, 141
reflectors
defined, 127
disadvantages of, 128
functions required of, 128
mrouted software, 129
sample program. *See*
Reflector.java sample
program
scenarios for running, 128
summary, 153
TCP in, 130
register packets, 161
register stop messages, 161

reliability
  multicast need for, 4
  summary, 152
  of TCP, 4
rendezvous points (RPs). *See* RPs
    (rendezvous points)
reuse option. *See* address reuse
    option
Reverse Path Forwarding (RPF)
    checks, 158
reverse shortest path trees, 158–159
robustness, 151
route optimization, 79–80
routers
  all-routers group, 96
  cores, 160–161
  forwarding state creation, 6
  grafting into forwarding trees, 6
  group awareness of, 5–6
  informing of group membership,
    5–6
  leaf, 5, 158–159
  querier routers, 156
  route optimization, 79–80
  RPs. *See* RPs (rendezvous points)
  SSM support, 78
RPs (rendezvous points), 79–80,
    156–157, 161–162, 165–166
RTCP (Real-Time Transport Control
    Protocol), 115–116
RTP (Real-Time Transport Protocol),
    115–116, 162

SAFI (Subsequent Address Family
    Identifier), 164
scalability
  application-level congestion
    control, 114–116
  complexity, trade-offs with, 3–4
  design notes, 125–126
  group size estimation, 125–126
  hidden station problem, 125–126
  Internet Robustness Principle, 115
  limitations on traffic, 114
  mping.c, test of, 113–114
  mping.c with congestion control,
    116–126
  multicast vs. unicast, 3
  NAK (negative acknowledgment)
    schemes, 115
  planning for volume, 114
  rate-limiting transmission,
    114–115
  recommendations for, 114
  reflector.java sample program,
    128–129
  RTP/RTCP, 115–116
  summary of problems with, 162
scope control
  administrative scoping, 89–90
  checking addresses, 171
  globally scoped addresses, 90, 93
  importance of, 88
  Java methods for, 93–94
  link local scope, 90
  local scope range, 89–90, 93
  multicast address space, 90–93

organizational local scope, 90
  TTL for, 15–17, 87–89
sdr (session directory) tool, 91, 162
selecting multicast addresses, 92–93,
    152
send packet functions, 170
senders, multicast
  C programming example, 18–20
  C# programming example, 58–61
  Java programming example,
    38–40, 49
  mping.c, function for, 104–105
  Reflector.java sample program,
    145–148
sending packets
  C# for, 52–61, 74
  C programming language, 17, 20
  Java, 37, 40
  .NET for, 52–61, 74
  Winsock function for, 32
service models, 155–157. *See also*
    ASM (Any Source Multicast);
    SSM (Source Specific Multicast)
Shared Ethernet, 3
shared trees, 160, 162
shortest paths, 156–157
sockets
  abstraction provided by, 1
  binding. *See* binding sockets
  closing. *See* closing sockets
  creating. *See* creating sockets
  defined, 9
  most common use of, 9
  TTL option. *See* TTL (Time-To-Live)
source discovery feature of SSM, 77,
    155
(source, group) pair notation, 78, 157
sparse mode, 88, 160–161
SSM (Source Specific Multicast)
  address range for, 92
  advanced C API, 82–84
  advantages of, 78–79
  any source option, 81
  ASM, compared to, 77–78
  C#, 70–71
  C API, 80–84
  C programming for, 31
  channels, 78, 157
  collision avoidance feature, 79
  controlled source option, 81–82
  defined, 77–78
  delta-based API, 80–82
  filtering feature, 79, 83
  full-state C API, 82–84
  host support for, 80
  IGMP with, 79–80, 156
  infrastructure reduction by, 79–80
  .NET platform, 84–85
  programming languages function
    table, 170–171
  protocol architectures, 155–156
  range of addresses for, 157
  route optimization feature, 79–80
  source discovery feature, 77, 155
  (source, group) pair notation, 78,
    157
  summary, 152

support for, 78
subscribing to groups. *See*
    membership in multicast
    groups, adding
Subsequent Address Family Identifier
    (SAFI), 164
summary of book, 151–153
Switched Ethernet, 3

TCP (Transmission Control Protocol)
  congestion control, 114
  disadvantages of, 4
  purpose of, 1
  reflectors using, 130
  sockets for, 9–10
thresholds, 88
topologies, 162, 163
trade-offs, power vs. complexity, 3–5
Transmission Control Protocol. *See*
    TCP (Transmission Control
    Protocol)
TTL scoping, 87–89
TTL (Time-To-Live)
  C#, 53–55, 73
  C programming language, 15–17,
    20
  defined in hops, 15
  Java, setting in, 37
  .NET, 53–55
  programming languages
    compared, 170
  scoping with, 87–89
  setting socket options, 15–16, 20
  summary, 151
  thresholds, 88
  tunneling, 17
  valid values, 15
tunneling, 17, 158, 163

UDP (User Datagram Protocol)
  advantages for multicast, 10
  API for, 9–10
  binding. *See* binding sockets
  congestion control, adding to, 4,
    114–115
  disadvantages for multicast, 4, 10
  lost packets in, 10
  purpose of, 1
  receiving packets, 10
  security issues, 4
  speed advantage, 10
  UdpClient class, 51–52, 71–76
unicast
  defined, 2
  reachability, 95–96
  scalability of, 3
unidirectional shared trees, 160

Winsock, 31–32